W9-ATZ-627

What Others Are Saying

"*All in My Head* is a great read! I thought the journal entries and descriptions of the 'roomies' were terrific. Also loved the lessons! It is a fantastic book and extremely helpful for anyone facing serious health challenges. It's authentic and hopeful without sugarcoating what the writer went through."

—Olivia Miller, author and publishing coach

"What an amazing story and journey. I was laughing at times and crying at others. I have a friend who was just diagnosed with cancer and will be starting daily chemo and radiation in the next few weeks. Can't wait to share this book with her. It is gripping and wonderful."

—Janice Desmond

"As the caregiver for my husband, a cancer survivor, I can relate to all the fear, sorrow, hope, happiness, *what nows* and *what ifs* that this writer went through. I thank her for sharing this story of her journey into hell and her incredible desire and determination to get back to the land of the living."

—Cathy DiCampo

"This book is amazing—filled with raw emotion, honesty, and just a lot of 'telling it like it is' moments. You don't have to have cancer to find it riveting."

—Gail Michael, author, California

"Marie Fricker leads her readers through the cancer battle and the impact of the illness in a way that will change their understanding of the disease forever."

—Greg Porell, editor, *South Shore Senior News*

"This book is a roller-coaster ride of fear, anxiety, and disappointment, along with humor, joy, and the author's unwavering desire to survive. My Kleenex was used for the sad, tough experiences as well as for laughing too much at some of the lines. Truly inspirational, not only to other cancer patients, but to everyone!"

—Stephanie Jenis, breast cancer survivor

"An honest and heartrending memoir that made me laugh and cry. It is a glorious and uplifting story and will be a huge source of hope to others."

—Phyllis Papani Godwin, CEO, Granite City Electric and Massachusetts business leader

"Marie Fricker's story is terrifying, inspiring, and heartwarming. She writes with honesty, and I know any cancer survivors would appreciate that as they struggle through their own journey. Her message of love and family and friends being most important is so true, and with her wit and humor, she gives so much life to her recovery."

—Nancy Brokamp

"This author's survival story, complete with her fears, joys, and, above all, faith, will go a long way in reassuring future patients that cancer is not a death sentence and that even a brain tumor can be vanquished."

—Ann Brandt, author and wife of a twenty-year PCNSL survivor

"What astonishes me are the details in the book about this writer's journey. As a cancer survivor myself, there is so much I don't remember. Clearly, Marie Fricker is authentic and honest about how brain cancer impacted her and her family. It's an incredible story."

—Beverly Comeau, Cancer Survivor

"Marie's gift for storytelling is evident throughout this memoir. Her entertaining and thought-provoking recounting of her experiences will resonate with those facing a similar challenge and their families."

—Carol Bulman, CEO/president, Jack Conway, Realtor

"As I read this book, I relived the PCNSL chapter of my own life. The writer shares her raw, authentic story with insights of light and humor. She takes the reader into the labyrinth of a journey with brain cancer and shows us that there is light at the end of the tunnel."

—Rev. Dr. Richard T. Rossiter, PCNSL survivor

"Marie, you are wonderful! I'm so happy you're going to share your story with the world."

—A personal note from Kris Carr, best-selling author of *Crazy Sexy Cancer Survivor* and *Crazy Sexy Cancer Tips*

ALL IN MY HEAD

HOW A HYPOCHONDRIAC BEAT BRAIN CANCER

Marie Fricker

ALL IN MY HEAD
Copyright © 2017 by Marie Fricker. All rights reserved.

No part of this publication may be reproduced, stored in a retrieval system or transmitted in any way by any means, electronic, mechanical, photocopy, recording or otherwise without the prior permission of the author except as provided by USA copyright law.

This book is designed to provide accurate and authoritative information with regard to the subject matter covered. This information is given with the understanding that neither the author nor Bluebullseye Press (a division of Bluebullseye LLC), is engaged in rendering legal, professional advice. Since the details of your situation are fact dependent, you should additionally seek the services of a competent professional.

This book is not intended as a substitute for the medical advice of physicians. The reader should regularly consult a physician in matters relating to his/her health and particularly with respect to any symptoms that may require diagnosis or medical attention.

In order to protect the privacy of some individuals in this book, the author has changed their names and identifying characteristics. Brand and product names are trademarks or registered trademarks of their respective owners.

PUBLISHED BY BLUEBULLSEYE PRESS
A division of Bluebullseye LLC
www.bluebullseyepress.com

Editorial advisor: Susan L. Roswit

Book cover design copyright © 2017 BookConnectors
Cover design by John H. Matthews
www.bookconnectors.com

Published in the United States of America

ISBN: 978-0-9975670-1-4
1. Biography & Autobiography / Personal Memoirs
2. Health & Fitness / Diseases / Cancer

To the heroes
Jason Fricker and Dr. Andrew Norden
and to the prize,
Benjamin James Kieffner

Acknowledgments

I HAVE ALWAYS hated the longwinded thank-you speeches of the Oscar winners on Academy Awards night in Hollywood. These motion picture icons express their appreciation to everyone from their costars and directors to the labor nurse who helped their mothers bring them into the world.

Yet as I think back on the many people who helped me battle cancer, as well as those who inspired and urged me to write this book, the list of shout-outs is going to be a tad long-winded. Feel free to turn the page if it gets to be too much to take, but even if the "get off the stage, you've said enough" music begins to play, I have to thank the following players in my journey for everything they did.

God, Jesus Christ, and the Blessed Mother for giving me a miraculous second chance.

The doctors and nurses of the Dana-Farber Cancer Institute and Brigham and Women's Hospital in Boston for doing much more than their jobs.

My husband, Al Fricker, my sister Elizabeth Lynch, my son Jason Fricker, and my daughter Allison Kieffner for bearing the brunt of me on the front lines. I love you all.

The following friends, family members, and neighbors for love, loyalty, rides, and food: William and Jessica Lynch; Thomas Lynch; Christine Fricker; Susan and Guido Fricker; Harry and Lorraine Fricker; Kelly Waterfield; Debbie Powers; Denise and Ted Bowes; Chris and Dino Fantegrossi; Sandy and John Ciulla; Susan Roswit; Joyce Wu; Carol Aylward; Barry Gates; Rev. Dr. Richard T. Rossiter; Tim Cummings; Chris Berlin; Ellen Golden; Louise Spillane; Dr. Mary Odegaard; Karen Fricker; Hospital Chaplain Heather Ramsay; Nursing Assistant Karlene Lewis; Brenda Russell; Elaine Bongarzone; Mark Fricker; and Stephanie Fricker, who can now stop asking, "Auntie Ree, when are you gonna write your book?"

Special appreciation to my smart, understanding, and infinitely patient editor, Andi Cumbo-Floyd, and to my expert advisors Hollis Gillespie and Gail Michael.

In closing (the exit music is deafening now), I want to thank all those people in my life who wrote their cell phone numbers on a yellow sticky pad next to my hospital bed for middle-of-the night panic calls. I never made the calls, but the list was a life raft, and they would have had to pry it out of my cold, dead hand to get it back.

And now for the most egregious offense of Oscar recipients' speeches on Academy Awards night—I want to thank my mother, Elizabeth Lee Gallishaw, for giving me a life that was so worth fighting for.

(If I've left anyone out in these acknowledgments, I'll have to play the cancer card and chalk it up to chemo brain. It doesn't mean that what you did for me is valued any less.)

Contents

Foreword

Marie Fricker has been my patient for eight years, which I reluctantly admit represents almost the entirety of my professional career as an attending physician. Marie didn't know it at the time, but I had completed my fellowship training in neuro-oncology just one year before I met her. I was experienced enough, however, to distinguish between a healthy person and a sick patient. When I first met Marie, she was sick. She was wearing an eye patch to prevent double vision, needed assistance to walk, and was convinced that she was imminently dying.

In fact, Marie was right. Although primary central nervous system lymphoma (PCNSL) is a very rare disease, untreated cases are rapidly fatal. Fortunately, this type of brain tumor is also highly treatable. For many patients, including Marie, chemotherapy treatment with methotrexate is effective and produces rapid neurological improvement. Over a period of months, I watched Marie transform from a sick patient into the dynamic, witty, outgoing, and fun person I know she was before her diagnosis.

With treatment now years in the past, she has returned to work, to her active social and family life, and, luckily for you, to her writing. She had begun to contemplate writing this book even as she lay in the hospital bed with methotrexate infusing into her veins. We joked that when the book was published and she became famous, she would bring me with her when she was interviewed on NBC's *Today* show.

Marie wanted to do something that would help future patients to cope with PCNSL and this book does exactly that. Marie's gift is the use of humor and colorful anecdotes to discuss her difficult and often terrifying journey. I am confident that you will enjoy reading her story, and if you or a loved one is currently suffering with any type of cancer, you will be inspired to stay positive, advocate for your needs, and use laughter as a coping strategy. Many patients are not as fortunate as Marie has proved to be over these past eight years, but every patient's quality of life can be improved by listening carefully to her message of perseverance and hope.

—Andrew Norden, MD
Dana Farber Cancer Institute
Boston, Massachusetts

Prologue

OUT OF THE blackness, the pounding comes in intervals—seven mind-numbing hammer beats, *BA BA BA BA BA BA BA*—followed by seven softer ones, *ba ba ba ba ba ba ba*.

Then a grinding drill sound, vibrating the slab beneath me. The ceiling is just inches from my face, but I close my eyes to pretend it isn't there, that I am not inside this coffin of an MRI scanning my brain for deadly lesions.

I am at death's door, and this tunnel is the entrance. How many more days, weeks can I survive?

What about my grandson? I won't live to see him walk. I want to hold him, love him.

Tears escape my eyes and flow down my cheeks.

A voice crackles in the darkness.

"Mrs. Fricker, don't move your head. We will have to take these pictures all over again if you move your head."

A Hot Foot

MY LEFT FOOT was hot, so hot that I had to stick it in a bucket of ice water for relief. And what was with these awful chills? My newborn grandson was awaiting a lifetime of spoiling, and I wanted to get at it. But something was wrong—very wrong.

Just two nights earlier, I had been waiting in the lobby of Brigham and Women's Hospital in Boston for a visitor's pass to go up to the labor room, where my daughter Alli was about to give birth to my first and much-anticipated grandchild. As my high heels clicked along the shiny parquet floor toward the elevators, I had no idea I'd be spending the next year of my life in this same building fighting to survive.

All I felt that night was excitement tinged by a bit of apprehension. So when a sudden wave of heat and knee-buckling weakness spread through my body, I attributed it to nerves. I sank down onto a brown suede couch in the lobby for a few minutes and took some deep breaths. When the feeling passed, I went up to join my daughter and her husband, Jeremy, for the big event. A ponytailed receptionist on the maternity floor directed me to the "Kieffner delivery room," and I went inside. Alli saw me immediately and reached for my hand.

"Mom, I can't take this anymore," she said while a monitor on a bedside stand showed the cresting wave of a contraction. Jeremy was standing close to her, huffing and puffing a breathing technique they had learned in childbirth classes, but she wasn't looking at him.

"How long has she been in this much pain?" I asked, pushing strands of my daughter's long blonde hair off her sweaty forehead.

"Almost six hours. They keep saying she can't have the epidural yet because it isn't time."

"Go ask them again, Mom," Alli pleaded as she slowly sank back in bed, as pale as the pillowcase behind her. "See if they'll give it to me now."

I went out into the hallway and cornered the nearest nurse.

"Please, can you help my daughter? She needs her epidural now. She's in terrible agony."

The nurse gave me a bored look, but a young, female doctor wearing blue scrubs brushed by her just then and came into the room. "Okay, Allison," she said as she prepared the needle, "you're about to start enjoying this journey a little more."

She numbed a spot on Alli's spine and then administered the miraculous anesthesia. Almost instantly, a smile spread across my daughter's face as she sat up and asked for a popsicle. There was another hour or so of labor, but no more pain.

At 4:00 a.m., Benjamin James Kieffner, weighing in at seven pounds and fourteen ounces, was pulled into the world looking blue and motionless. For two seconds, none of us breathed until he shot a lobster-red fist in the air and wailed. As he was cleaned up and placed on Alli's chest, she looked into his watery blue eyes with hers and said, "Hi, buddy."

Jeremy was hovering over them and wiping away tears. He was too afraid to hold the baby yet, but I wasn't. When a nurse swaddled Ben in a blue cotton blanket and placed him on my lap, I knew this boy was mine, and I was his. He looked directly at me, which was a pretty advanced act for a newborn.

"Hello, Benji James, I am your grandmother," I said, returning his steady gaze. "I'm not sure what you're going to call me yet, but just know that I love you and that I'll do anything for you for the rest of my life."

When I spoke those words to my firstborn grandchild, I couldn't have foreseen the frightening turn of events that was about to happen to me in just a matter of days and that "the rest of my life" might, in fact, be a very short time.

I drove home from the hospital as the sun was rising on a picture-perfect fall day in Boston. I should have felt calm and happy. Benjamin was healthy and Alli was fine, so why was I still so nervous? My face was clammy, and my hands were gripping the steering wheel. I was no stranger to anxiety, but what was causing it now when all was well?

The next day, my husband Al and I, along with an entourage of family members, went to visit Alli and the baby at the hospital, but I felt really out of it. My head was foggy, my ears were blocked, and I had terrible chills but no fever, which was weird. I didn't want to be around Ben if something was coming on, so I stayed for a few minutes and then went home to rest.

As I walked into the house, I threw my pocketbook on the bench in the hall, and that's when I felt it: an intense burning sensation in my left foot. It wasn't red or warm to the touch, just sizzling hot from inside. Along with the heat, a feeling of pins and needles was spreading all the way up to my knee. For the next two days, I spent most of my time on the couch or sitting at the computer with my foot in a yellow plastic bucket filled with ice water. I was searching for an answer to my symptoms—hot foot, chills with no fever, numbness on one side—but Google wasn't coming up with anything.

On the morning of the third day when I was feeling worse than ever, Al walked into the room as I sat at the computer.

"Something is really wrong with me," I said. "I'm getting weaker by the minute, and I can't stop shaking."

"Are you sure you're not overreacting, Ree?" asked my nonalarmist husband. "You always think the worst."

"No, this is different, Al. I think it's really bad."

"And when have you not thought that?" He smiled teasingly.

He had a point there. I had a long history of hypochondria and had diagnosed myself with everything from hoof and mouth disease to cholera over the years. The medical symptoms book that lived on my nightstand was dog-eared from overuse.

Yet this time I was getting worse by the day. On day 4, Al decided to take me to the ER at the same hospital where my daughter had just given birth. He still didn't believe I had anything serious, but he wanted to put an end to my worrying and restore peace to the house.

"Don't tell Alli that we're going to the emergency room," I said as we arrived in the Brigham and Women's parking lot on a cold and rainy Tuesday night. "I don't want her to worry. She's just had a baby."

The ER was lined wall to wall with people in various stages of distress—limping, moaning, and dripping blood.

"Oh great, we're gonna be here forever," said Al, whose biggest stressor in life was waiting in line—at the grocery store, the bank, a movie theater, or in traffic. He could endure the latter only when he was working at his job as a tractor trailer driver for Stop & Shop. "I don't mind being stuck in gridlock on the highway with the big rig," he'd say, "because at least I'm getting paid for it."

Heaving an annoyed sigh, he sat down in a blue leather chair as I checked in with an elderly volunteer at the front counter. The TVs in the room were broadcasting some kind of a verbal sparring match between Obama and McCain, who were about to battle it out for the presidency one month later. Normally, I would have loved watching this, but I was so weak that I just leaned against Al's shoulder as he put his arm around me and picked up a newspaper.

When my name was finally called, I followed a nurse into an exam room surrounded by a green-and-white checked curtain. I hated hospitals, and my nerves were already on edge. A young Nordic-looking doctor slid back the curtain and introduced himself.

"Would you tell me your date of birth please?" he asked.

"6-27-53." I didn't know it then, but those numbers—6-27-53—would become my moniker for the next year or more in this same hospital.

"Okay, now smile, follow my finger with your eyes, and push back when I try to press your knee down."

"Am I having a stroke?" I asked at the end of his exam.

"No," he said with a laugh. "I really don't think there's anything wrong with your brain, Mrs. Fricker. You probably just have a virus. See your doctor if you don't feel better soon."

Someone directed me back to the waiting room, where I found my husband with his head back and mouth open, asleep in his chair.

"They don't know what's wrong with me," I said as we walked out into the rain to the parking garage. "They think it's a virus. What am I going to do, Al? I can't go on like this."

"Okay, calm down, Ree," he said as he started his old but reliable 2004 Ford Explorer. "Maybe they're right, and it's just some kind of a nasty bug. Let's give it another week or so before you panic."

Al was a stoic (wouldn't complain if he was on life support) type of guy, and he wanted to put an end to all this. His parents were German and Latvian immigrants who had escaped from their countries under gunfire during WWII and had taught their four kids to never show fear.

Unfortunately, their second son, Elmar (Al to his American peers) had made a fateful late-night trip to a cheap bar in Cambridge on January 19 of 1973. He was a fabulous piano and keyboard player and had played in the band that was performing there that night. Wearing a brown leather jacket and steel-rimmed glasses, he'd asked a girl in a miniskirt and high boots for her phone number and married her three years later. Fear had just officially entered this man's life.

In the three days that followed our trip to the emergency room, I spent hours on my sofa, wrapped in an electric blanket to quell my teeth-chattering chills. The pins and needles I had felt from my foot to my knee had now spread all the way up to my thigh. And suddenly, the left side of my upper lip felt like it had been shot with Novocaine.

My twenty-six-year old son Jason (Jay), a paramedic and firefighter, had been listening to my litany of symptoms since the whole thing had begun six days earlier.

"I know you're a wicked neurotic, Mom," he said one morning. "But you don't look so good, and I don't like that your problems are all on one side. I'm going to take you back to the ER."

Like the movie *Groundhog Day*, the scenario was much the same. We went, and we waited. A doctor concluded,

"Probably a virus, but just to be sure, I'm referring you to a neurologist if these symptoms persist."

Jay tried to be upbeat on the drive back to the house as he chewed on a piece of the Nicorette gum to which he had become more addicted than he was to the smoking habit he was trying to kick.

"I don't know, Ma. If you were having a stroke or something, they would see that. Maybe I've just caught your hypochondria."

We both laughed, but neither of us was amused.

Toughing It Out

THE NEXT MORNING, feeling no better but wanting desperately to function, I decided to try to go to work. I was the advertising director for a large real estate company, and I had already taken five days off. I knew my colleagues thought I was just using the time to be with the new baby, but I hadn't even seen Ben since the symptoms began. I was too afraid that I might have something contagious.

As much of a worrier as I have always been, I was never one to give in to myself when it came to my job. Fevers, coughs, even pounding migraines never stopped me from showing up for duty. I would stick out a headache all day long and then throw up in a plastic bag on the drive home.

I attributed this work ethic to my father, Henry Gallishaw, a rail-thin man who suffered from rheumatoid arthritis and congestive heart disease—both the aftereffects of a childhood bout of rheumatic fever twenty years before penicillin was even a gleam in Alexander Fleming's eye. As sickly as he was, he never missed a day of work unless he was having open-heart surgery, which he did three times.

I remember sitting at the kitchen table swinging my black Mary Jane shoes and eating a bowl of Cheerios one morning while my mother pleaded with my father not to go back to work so soon after one of his operations. "Henry, you're pushing yourself way too hard," she said. "You need a little more time to get your strength back."

"Don't worry about it, dear, I can always catch a ride home in the hearse," he said, winking at me as he grabbed his brown lunch bag off the counter. "Let this be a lesson to you, daughter [he often called me "daughter" when something profound was about to be said]. You always show up for work. You don't let your company down. Remember, they can easily replace you. And then who's gonna buy the Purina Dog Chow?"

I had always been driven to "show up"—both at college, where I earned a bachelor's and master's degree, and in my career. For the last fifteen years, I had been managing the advertising department at the Jack Conway Real Estate Company, a firm with thirty-eight sales offices from Boston to Cape Cod. I loved working closely with the founder and chairman of the board, who at eighty-five years old had an idea a minute and moved faster than I did.

Smart and driven, Jack Conway demanded much from his employees, especially me. I was always under the stress of trying to devise a new campaign or idea to impress him. He had little tolerance for mistakes but was quick to offer praise when praise was due. In 2006, I produced a documentary about the company's fiftieth anniversary entitled *The House That Jack Built*. The video was a big hit and went on to win six national communications awards. When I arrived at work on the day the first trophy was delivered, Jack had gathered everyone in the lobby to greet me.

"Let's have three cheers for our award-winning movie producer, Cecilia B. DeFricker," he said in his booming, ringmaster's voice, equating me with the legendary Hollywood director Cecil B. DeMille. Then he held his two fists in the air and led the group in a rousing triple chorus of "Hip, hip, hooray." One "hip, hip, hooray" meant that Jack was mildly pleased with something you did, but three meant that he was exhilarated, and I got the hat trick that day.

Of course, there were other days when the same booming voice was bellowing at me for something I had done wrong, so that made the little victories all the sweeter. Working for Jack Conway was a roller-coaster ride, but I never would have swapped it for the merry-go-round of a less challenging environment.

Since my illness had begun, I had really missed my job, and despite the fact that I wasn't feeling any better, I decided to tough it out and go to work on a Friday morning.

Dick Cahill, our company president, a big, ruddy-faced man who was always dressed to the nines, was sitting at the conference table in my office when I arrived. He was wearing a pale blue suit jacket with a crisp white shirt and pink tie.

"Marie, put on your thinking cap," he said. "I need a blockbuster marketing package for a new condo development that we're trying to land. Give me something that will blow everybody else out of the park and get us this contract."

I stared at the tassels on Dick's brown leather loafers as he discussed the details of the project and explained what he needed from the ad department. I nodded a few times and pretended to be interested, but I was too weak to concentrate on a word he was saying. All I wanted to do was go home and lie down. I left at noon.

Lesson learned: When something is really wrong, you can't always just tough it out.

Not a Virus

Two days after my failed attempt to return to work, I drove to the 5:00 p.m. Mass at St. Jerome's Church in Weymouth, which was my routine on a Sunday night. It wasn't my parish, but it was the only one that offered a late Mass, and early mornings have never been my thing.

I found the closest spot in the crowded church parking lot and slid into the pew nearest to the door in case I needed to exit quickly. A big-bellied priest in purple and white robes was leading a prayer, but my ears were so blocked that I couldn't hear a word he was saying. After a while, the effort of standing up and kneeling felt like climbing Mount Everest.

I left my seat and walked through the "baby's crying room" and into the tiny green-walled bathroom at the back of the church. I splashed water on my face and looked in the mirror. My complexion was gray even though I was wearing makeup, and I felt like I was hearing from inside a tunnel.

I couldn't ask Al or Jay to take me to another emergency room, so I decided to drive myself into the Massachusetts Eye and Ear Infirmary in Boston. I knew they had an urgent care clinic on the weekends, and I was hoping that this mystery illness was some kind of middle ear infection. I just wanted to have a diagnosis, get some antibiotics, and get on with my life.

I left the church, where the organist was playing "One Bread, One Body" as people noisily kicked back their kneeling pads to go up for communion, and drove the twenty minutes into Boston with barely any traffic. After parking in the hospital's garage, I checked into the clinic and got called right away.

"Your ears are normal, Mrs. Fricker," said a short, dark-bearded doctor after conducting a wide range of "raise your hand when you hear this" tests. "Have you had a flu shot this year?"

"Please don't go there," I snapped. "This is not the flu, and it's not a virus. I am getting worse every day."

"All I can tell you is that your ears are not the issue," he said, walking me toward the door. "Follow up with your own physician if you don't improve."

What a waste of time, I thought, *coming all the way in here and still having no answers.*

I trudged back to my car and was driving home when the white lines on the highway suddenly doubled, and I couldn't tell where one lane ended and the other began. I have no idea how I made it back to my house that night, but by the grace of God, I did. When I got home, the TV in my living room had an identical twin as did my husband and everything else I looked at. I had double vision, and I was scared.

The next day, my sister Betty, who is eight years my senior and my only sibling, took me to see my own doctor, a sweet and caring woman I had chosen for her bedside manner. I told Dr. Olson about the numbness, the lethargy, the three emergency room visits, and the new double vision. When she heard the last item on the checklist, her expression changed from "Oh, you're fine" to "Oh no, what's wrong with you?"

"Marie, I don't know of any virus that causes double vision," she said. "I want you to have an MRI today, just to rule out anything bad. And then if the symptoms continue, you won't be so worried."

My sister went off to a waiting room as I was led to the MRI area, where I changed into a blue-and-white johnny and got hoisted onto a narrow slab. I was petrified to enter the dark tunnel of the scanner but desperate enough to do it. Betty would later tell me, "I knew it was bad when I heard your doctor being paged." I'm glad she didn't tell me that then.

"Here, Mrs. Fricker, squeeze this ball in the event of an emergency," said a slim red-haired nurse as she placed a small rubber ball in my hand and closed my fingers around it. She went back into the scanning area and said through a loudspeaker, "Go ahead. Squeeze the ball now, please."

I did, and she gave me the thumbs-up sign.

Claustrophobia set in the minute I entered the black tube, but I fought off the urge to scream and wondered if going stark raving mad would count as an emergency.

After twenty minutes of clanging, buzzing, and jack-hammer noises, as well as something that sounded like a whooping Apache war cry in the old Western movies, I felt my slab being pulled from the machine.

"Don't move, please," said a doctor who was now standing next to me. "I am going to inject you with some contrast dye and take some more pictures." He said it so cheerfully like, "I just want to get a few more shots for my Facebook page." But he averted his eyes when I asked, "Do you see anything? Am I okay?"

When the scanning was over, a nurse helped me down from the table, and everything around me—walls, machines, and furniture—suddenly seemed to be floating above the floor. I had to close one eye to see my way back to the changing room.

White Spots

Dr. Olson called me at home that night. "Marie, I have good news and bad news," she said. "The MRI showed two white spots in your brain—a 1.5 centimeter lesion in your thalamus and a smaller one in your right frontal lobe."

This can't possibly be the good news, I thought.

"You don't have a brain tumor, and you didn't have a stroke, but we think you have multiple sclerosis."

"Multiple sclerosis. Oh my god." I sank onto the couch.

"Now don't panic," she said. "The symptoms you're having right now are known as a flare-up. I'm going to send you to a neurologist tomorrow who will give you a steroid shot, and you will feel much better. People with MS live nearly normal lives today."

MS—didn't that happen to young people? I was fifty-five years old!

"It's going to be okay," said Al when I told him the diagnosis. "Try to get some sleep now. We'll deal with this together. You have a lot of people who love you, including me."

"But you said it was nothing, that I was overreacting, imagining the worst," I said.

"I know I did, Ree," he said, hugging me. "I really believed that based on the past. I should have taken you more seriously."

I cried myself to sleep that night, picturing my friend Sally's sister, an MS victim who had lived a slowly degenerating existence and ended up unable to walk, talk, or feed herself.

Give Me the 'Roids!

THE NEXT MORNING, Betty and I drove to the office of Dr. Wilson, a prominent neurologist in Boston. He was a thin man in his fifties with sparse hair, wire-rimmed glasses, and a stern face.

"Hello, Mrs. Fricker. Can you please hold your arms out to the sides and then touch your fingers to your nose with your eyes closed," he said. "That's it. Now follow my finger—that's right. When I lift your leg, I want you to push back and try to stop me. Now the same thing with your arm. Push back."

At this point, just eight days since Ben's birth, I was so weak that I was sitting in a wheelchair that Betty had stolen from the hallway, and my nerves were totally shot. When Dr. Wilson finished his exam, I said, "Can you give me the steroids now? I really need them."

He took his glasses off and stared at me. "I don't think you have multiple sclerosis, Mrs. Fricker," he said matter-of-factly. "And I'm not going to treat something when I don't know what it is. This could even be a lymphoma. I won't give you steroids or any other medication until I know what you have."

"But please, I really need help," I said, grabbing his sleeve. "They said you'd give me a steroid shot, and I'd feel better." I was so desperate at this point that the word *lymphoma* hadn't even registered with me.

He pulled away and straightened his shoulders. "Mrs. Fricker, do you hear what I'm saying to you? These lesions on your scans are quite possibly cancer. I'll bet the tumor is putting pressure on your eye, and that's why you're having double vision."

My sister gripped my hand.

"Dr. Wilson, I am a very anxious woman, and you are scaring the hell out of me," I said. "Are you saying I have a brain tumor?"

"That would be my guess, but more tests will have to be done."

His demeanor was detached, almost annoyed. As terrified as I was, I looked him squarely in the eyes, even though I was seeing four of them. "Whatever is wrong with me, you will not be my doctor," I said.

He looked taken aback. "Do you want me to lie to you, Mrs. Fricker?"

"No, but I want to be assigned to a doctor who is known for compassion. Is there anyone like that at the hospital?"

"Yes, me," he said.

"No, anyone but you."

"I'm going to take your scans to the head radiologist at Brigham and Women's Hospital and have him look at them. Please wait in my office until I call in the results of our consultation."

A nurse directed us through a set of glass doors back to the waiting room. After a while, she came back and said that the doctor was on the phone and would like to talk with my sister.

Betty was led away to take the call in his office. She related the conversation to me later.

"As I suspected, we think Mrs. Fricker has lymphoma, not MS," said Dr. Wilson in his blunt manner.

"Oh my god," said Betty. "Is that a death sentence?"

"It's treatable. I'll arrange to have her admitted today."

She tried to ask another question, but he had hung up.

As I looked through the glass doors from the waiting room, I could see Betty walking back toward me. Her shoulders were slouched and her face worn with a mixture of fear and worry. But before she opened the door that led to where I was sitting, I saw her straighten her back and put a confident look on her face. She didn't want me to know how scared she was. In her usual big-sister manner, she was protecting me.

Under the Microscope

I WAS ADMITTED to Brigham and Women's Hospital (the Brigham) and assigned, as requested, not to Dr. Wilson but to a more pleasant neurologist named Dr. Macey. He was a smiling, middle-aged man with a salt-and-pepper bouffant hairstyle that reminded me of a 1940s movie idol. Since this was a teaching hospital, he was constantly trailed by a team of young neurology residents—four men and one woman— who were eager to study my unusual case. I really didn't care about the "guinea pig" aspect of my condition, just as long as somebody, anybody, could make me feel better. If the custodian wanted to kick in a remedy, I'd have taken it.

I spent the next two weeks as an inpatient at the Brigham, getting poked, prodded, and stuffed into machines for scans, spinal taps, and blood draws. At the same time, I was on a definite downward slope. Within days of my admission, I needed a walker and a nurse's help to get from my bed to the bathroom.

One night during this barrage of diagnostic testing, Dr. Macey showed up alone in my room flashing a tight grin. "Well, Mrs. Fricker, it looks like we may not be dealing with a cancer situation at all," he said. "Your tests have all come back nonconclusive for lymphoma. You may actually have a rare demyelinating [nerve-stripping] disease that will resolve itself in time."

I couldn't believe the words coming out of this man's mouth—not cancer? Could I possibly have dodged the deadly bullet that Wilson had suspected? My sister-in-law Lorraine called just as he was leaving, and I shared the good news with her. She was elated, and I slept soundly for the first time in weeks. Unfortunately, Dr. Macey's theory was later proven wrong, but I still thank him for that one night of hope.

As the days went by in the hospital, I knew that whatever was in my brain was getting bigger and bolder, and it was bad—very bad. No one could feel like this and go on living very long. The double vision was worse, the lethargy was worse, and my ability to do basic things like type an e-mail took every ounce of my strength to accomplish, with my head and shoulders bent completely over the keyboard.

"This must be what death feels like," I told my sister on one of her visits. My left eye was drooping, and the numbness and buzzing on my left side were almost unbearable. I spent nearly all my time praying to God, Jesus, the Blessed Mother, and my own mother, who had died twenty-three years before that. Someone had to hear me, and maybe someone would answer.

Help! Somebody? Anybody?

ONE MORNING, DURING a going-nowhere session of "Why me?" I looked up to see a young woman with platinum-blonde hair and glasses standing at the foot of my bed.

"Hello, Mrs. Fricker. My name is Ellen Golden," she said. "I'm a social worker at the hospital, and I'd like to talk with you about the support services you may need when you go home."

Home—did that place even still exist? I felt like I had been in the hospital for months, but it had really only been eight days. She was offering things like walkers, home health aides, and visiting nurses, and I said *yes* to all of them. I wanted anything and anyone who could help me feel better.

In the days and weeks that followed, Ellen often dropped by my room and listened to my litany of fears. It usually ended with "What am I going to do, Ellen? Do you think I'm going to die?"

"No, I don't," she'd say. "The doctors are going to figure out what's wrong with you, and then they'll be able to do something about it. You're right where you should be right now. You just have to try to calm down."

Ellen had an abundance of patience, and my foggy brain was beginning to think she might actually be an angel.

Unfortunately, she wasn't the only hospital employee who had to deal with my constant pleas for reassurance. "Do you think I'm going to live?" was a question I was asking everyone—from head doctors to candy stripers to anyone else within earshot. I'll never forget the frightened looks on the faces of some of my Haitian personal care attendants, who would laugh nervously and pretend they didn't speak English.

After fifteen days of exhaustive testing, including spinal taps, MRIs, pet scans, and blood draws, no conclusive diagnosis had been made.

PCNSL—What the Hell?

"We still don't know for sure what you have, Mrs. Fricker, but we believe it is probably a highly rare lymphoma of the brain," said Dr. Macey one morning. "These tumors have their own blood supply, so they are definitely not good guys."

The thought of some insidious growth inside my brain having its own blood supply made me want to vomit. Was I in some kind of horror movie where I was taken over by an alien mass with its own goddamn blood supply?

"Why are you referring to the spots on my MRI as tumors?" I asked. "Before they called them *lesions*. Can't you just call them *lesions*?"

"Sure, if that makes you feel better, I'll refer to them as *lesions*."

For some reason, it did.

"The disease that we suspect you have is called primary central nervous system lymphoma, acronym PCNSL," said Dr. Macey. "All of your tests have shown no tumors anywhere else in your body, which is why it's called primary, having originated in your brain and not traveled there from someplace else."

"You said *tumor* again."

"The problem is that we can't treat you for anything without a positive diagnosis," he said, pushing back an errant strand of his precisely coiffed hair. "All of our tests—the lumbar punctures, blood work, and scans—have been inconclusive."

He put his hand on my shoulder as he turned to leave. "Don't worry, Mrs. Fricker. We'll get to the bottom of this."

Crippled by fear and lethargy, I spent most of my time curled in the fetal position facing a wall. I knew this wasn't fair to some of my visitors, who had traveled long distances to see me, but I was already in another realm of existence from healthy people, and I couldn't bridge the gap. There was a hollowness in my head that felt like I was at the bottom of a mine shaft listening to voices fading in and out from the surface.

My coworker Louise, a tiny woman with short brown curly hair, dropped by one night after a steady stream of visitors had finally departed. I have always liked Louise, but I couldn't possibly interact with anyone else. "I can't talk with you," I said, too weak to even pretend. "It's not you, Louise, I just can't talk."

"So don't talk," she said. "I'll just read my magazine." She picked up papers and wrappers from the floor near my bed, arranged my slippers neatly in a row, and threw a half-eaten bagel into the wastebasket. Then she opened an issue of *Cosmopolitan* that someone had brought me and read it silently. I never spoke a word to her, but there was something oddly comforting about her quiet presence next to my bed. About an hour later, Jay arrived to bring me some clean pajamas.

"Oh, hi, Louise, long time no see," he said, walking over to her.

"Oh my god, Jason, you are all grown up and so handsome," she said, giving him a hug. "And I heard all about you becoming a firefighter and a paramedic. That's awesome. Well, since your mother has company now, I'm going to take off."

She walked over to me and took one of my hands in both of hers. "I'm praying for you, Marie," she said. "God's not going to let anything happen to someone that has a new grandbaby to spoil."

I think I said, "Thanks for coming, Louise," but I'm really not sure.

Shove Me on a Plane

DURING THIS TIME, the TV news was filled with reports of our US Senator Ted Kennedy, who was being treated for a recently diagnosed brain tumor. One afternoon Jay brought me a copy of a *Boston Globe* article about Ted convening the best heads in medicine to confer about the treatment of his glioblastoma. The piece ended with, "Mr. Kennedy, seventy-six, flew to Durham, North Carolina. There, at Duke University on June 2, neurosurgeons operated for three and a half hours and declared the procedure successful."

"Jay, you've got to take me to see Ted's doctor," I said. "Maybe he'll know what I have and can help me. Please call him or get an ambulance and put me on a plane."

While he balked at the suggestion of shoving my body onto a jumbo jet to North Carolina, my son did write a phenomenal letter to Dr. Allan Friedman, the head surgeon on Kennedy's case. His note ended with, "Every day my mother's symptoms are progressing. She is a very nervous woman and is really at the end of her rope. We are in desperate need of help. She was a vibrant, healthy person, and this illness came on so quickly and has been so debilitating. She has full insurance, and we could fly out to you immediately. Any help or advice you could offer would be greatly appreciated."

About a week later, Dr. Friedman wrote back to Jay, asking him to forward all my MRI scans and records to him, but by then I had a diagnosis, and the battle had begun.

Enter Hero—Stage Right

I WAS LYING facedown in my hospital bed one morning when someone tapped my right shoulder. I rolled over and saw a thin young man smiling at me with a mouthful of impeccable white teeth. He was mostly bald, and was wearing frameless glasses and a white lab coat with a stethoscope around his neck.

"Mrs. Fricker, I'm Dr. Andrew Norden, the neuro-oncologist assigned to your case," he said, extending his hand to me. His name badge said "Dana-Farber Cancer Institute." That was Brigham and Women's oncology affiliate, which was connected to the hospital by an indoor bridge.

Even wearing an eye patch to stop my double vision, I could see that this person was young, too young to be a doctor.

"How old are you?" I asked, grabbing his hand and holding on to it. (I've never had much tact, but in my current condition, my filter level was zero.)

"I'm thirty-two," he said.

Holy mother of God, they had sent a boy to deal with a dying woman.

"Why can't you be forty-two?" I asked.

He laughed. "Oh, come on, you wouldn't want me to be burnt out, would you?"

"Have you ever had a patient with this disease that they think I have—this PCNSL?" I asked.

"Yes," he said, fingering his stethoscope nervously and looking down for a second.

"How many?"

"I don't know. More than ten, but less than twenty."

"So eleven, right?"

"Yes."

OMG, this Doogie Howser was young and inexperienced, but he was all I had.

"Please don't let me die, Dr. Norden," I said.

"If your diagnosis is lymphoma, your cancer is treatable," he said. "My goal is to cure you."

That last statement was to become my life raft in a sea of despair. I wrote it down on a napkin and held on to it through seventeen chemo treatments, hair loss, allergic reactions, and days and nights of sheer terror.

A few days after I met him, Dr. Norden told me that the only way to positively diagnose my illness was through a brain biopsy. A prominent surgeon had been selected for the task, and all I had to do was give him my consent. Dr. Billings was a tall, good-looking man with an air of bravado, and he laid out the risks of the surgery to me and my family.

"I'm going to try to get a piece of tissue from the small lesion in your frontal lobe," he said. "But if I can't do it, I'll have to go for the larger one in your thalamus, which is deep in your brain, and has the risk of causing deficits. Even so, I've done biopsies of that area before, and I'm pretty confident of success."

"We don't want her to have it," said my sister. "What if she comes out of it paralyzed or blind?" Betty was a master of the what-ifs for every situation in life, so I wasn't surprised to hear her bring up a few heavy-duty ones.

The surgeon pointed at me as I sat slumped over in my wheelchair with my eye patch. "Look at her," he said. "The deficits are already here, and they will get worse every day."

"Just do it," I said, silencing both of them. "Do the biopsy. I can't live like this."

Fright Night

ONE OF MY favorite holidays—Halloween—was chosen for the ghoulish task of boring into my brain with a power drill. My "costume" was a tall metal cage that was being screwed into my skull while I was under local anesthesia. Standing beside the doctor who was attaching it to me was a technician from the company that made it.

After much struggle and several failed attempts, the doctor turned to the other man with an angry glare. "The screws don't fit," he said.

The technician examined them. "You're right," he said. "They are for an older model of this device, not this one."

There was tension in the air, but I wasn't worried. Under the peaceful effect of a tranquilizing drip, I said, "Maybe someone should go to the hardware store and pick up some more screws."

No one replied.

Eventually, the issue was resolved, and I was wheeled into the operating room with headgear in place. People were milling about and talking as I grabbed the sleeve of the nearest nurse. "I can hear you," I said. "I'm still awake. Aren't I supposed to be asleep in here? I need more anesthesia."

Someone must have obliged, and blackness descended.

I found out later that there had been several emergencies at the hospital that night, and my biopsy had been delayed for hours, but no one had informed my family. My husband, sister, children, and two nephews were waiting anxiously for news that the surgery was over, and they were beginning to think that something had gone terribly wrong.

When the phone finally rang in the waiting room, Jay was elected to answer it. As young as he was, he was the leader in this journey from day one and was my medical proxy. He repeated the conversation to me later.

"Hello, Jason, your mother made it through the surgery fine and is in the recovery room," said Dr. Billings. "I was able to get the tissue from the smaller lesion in the frontal lobe, so I didn't need to go for the thalamus. We'll have to wait for the pathology report now, but I've seen a lot of these tumors, and I'm pretty sure we're looking at a lymphoma."

"Thank you, Doctor. Can we see her now?"

"Soon, but just briefly. She's in the recovery room ICU."

Jay told me that my family's immediate reaction was a mixture of relief that I had made it through the surgery and sheer terror that brain cancer had virtually been confirmed. They made their way up the two flights to the recovery room and were allowed in when I started to wake up.

"Am I alive?" I asked from a mental haze as the anesthesia started to wear off. I could vaguely hear my kids saying "Mom" but couldn't answer them. Jay told me that I reached for Alli's hand when she called out to me, but not his, which validated his long-held theory that I liked her better. I had a tube down my throat, and the left side of my face was drooping like Silly Putty. As a paramedic, my son had seen a lot of critically ill patients, and for the first time, he actually thought I might die.

He walked back to the parking garage praying for a sign from above that I would be all right. Only recently did he tell me about what happened to him that night. "As I put my key in the ignition, I suddenly felt this incredible wave of love and protection sweep over me," said Jay. "I can't describe it, but it was like nothing I've ever experienced in my life, and I knew I was no longer alone in my truck. I sensed a presence in the passenger seat, but it was so overwhelming that I was too afraid to look in that direction. I just stared straight ahead and drove out of the garage. But from that moment on, I knew that you were not going to die."

Walking the Plank

DESPITE JAY'S NEW optimistic outlook, my condition plummeted in the days after the biopsy. I was disoriented and unable to walk without people on both sides of me, usually my nephews, Billy and Tom.

"Come on, Auntie Ree," one of them would say. "It's time for a hike to the elevators and back. It's gonna be a blast."

On one of these excursions, a little boy was walking down the hall toward us with his mother. He pointed up at my eye patch and said, "Look, Mommy, it's a lady pirate."

"Shhh," said the mother, apologizing to me. I would have smiled at her if my mouth still remembered how to do that.

The nurses were giving me daily injections of heparin to prevent blood clots, which they were shooting into the left side of my stomach because that side of my body was so numb by now that I couldn't even feel the needle going in. The only evidence of getting the shots was the mottled field of black and blue growing on one side of my belly.

A few days after the biopsy, my old friend and social worker Ellen Golden dropped in to say hello. I grabbed her hand as she sat beside me. "Ellen, I'm so much worse. If I drop something on the floor, it's gone forever in a bottomless pit. I feel like I'm inside a deep well and everyone else is at the surface. When I try to cut my food, I'm stabbing at it from the wrong side of the plate. What am I going to do?"

She put her hand on my shoulder and stared into my eyes. "Of course, you're feeling worse, Marie. You've just had brain surgery." She put down her clipboard and sprang into action, straightening out my bed, clearing clutter from my windowsill, removing my breakfast tray, holding my glass of ginger ale while I sipped from it, and placing magazines within my reach.

It was comforting to watch her swift, take-charge actions as she went about the business of meeting my needs and talking to me in her soft, soothing tone. She was an angel of mercy and, in my rattled mind, quite possibly a saint.

Just the Facts, Ma'am

THE PATHOLOGY REPORT was due to come in within ten days after the biopsy, and I was petrified. What if it wasn't this lymphoma of the brain? What if it was the same tumor that Ted Kennedy was dying from right now? What if it was too far gone for treatment?

One week after the surgery, Kelly, my friend and coworker, was visiting me when Dr. Norden came into my room carrying the results of the biopsy. Kelly got up to leave, but I asked her to stay. She took my hand as Dr. Norden talked.

"It's what we expected—non-Hodgkin's large B-cell lymphoma—PCNSL," he said. "And the good news is we can now do something about it. Your first chemotherapy treatment is scheduled for tomorrow."

And so it was. A previously healthy, moderately overweight middle-aged woman who never smoked or drank had just been officially told that she had brain cancer. It wasn't high blood pressure, kidney stones, or an overactive thyroid; it was brain cancer.

"Dr. Norden, do you think I'll live long enough to see my grandson walk?" I asked, fighting off the fear.

"Yes, I think so."

"Will I see him go to kindergarten?"

"I really can't answer that."

I shot an anxious glance at Kelly, who asked, "How big are the tumors, Doctor?"

"No, don't tell me," I said in a panic. "I don't want to know."

"Don't worry, Marie," said Dr. Norden, squeezing my shoulder before he left the room. "We're in this together."

Kelly, a bubbly blonde-haired forty-four-year-old with the body of a teenager, launched into a supportive discourse on "you can beat this thing" and gratefully departed when the nurse came in to take my vitals.

And then I did something I never should have. I took out my laptop and Googled my illness. "Primary Central Nervous System Lymphoma (acronym PCNSL)—A rare form of brain cancer that occurs in only about 30 out of 10 million people, mostly in the immune-compromised population of HIV/AIDS patients."

Because of its rarity, not a lot of research had been done on this disease, and statistics were scant and horrifying. According to *Wikipedia*, "The median survival is 10 to 18 months in immuno-competent patients, and less in those with AIDS. The addition of methotrexate and leucovorin [which would be my prescribed course of treatment] may extend survival to a median of 3.5 years."

I couldn't read any more. I wouldn't be able to breathe if I read one more word.

The Inquisition

SHORTLY AFTER MY biopsy results came in, Dr. Norden asked me if I would agree to be the subject of a hospital procedure known as the "Chief's Rounds." I said yes, not even knowing what it was.

"It's a process that's done when we get an unusual case like yours," he explained. "The head of our neurology department and about twenty-five doctors and residents will ask you about how your illness presented itself and then guess at what kind of tumor you have before reading the pathology report—the answer sheet, so to speak."

"Sounds like a fun game, for everyone but me, but sure, I'll do it. I've got nothing better to do."

When the day came for the Chief's Rounds, wearing only a johnny and some slipper socks, I was wheeled into a huge wood-paneled conference room. I should have asked for a bathrobe, but I was too sick to care.

As anticipated, the doctors asked me a barrage of questions. They made me tell my story, from the hot foot through all the emergency room visits to the double vision and my misdiagnosis with MS. For some reason, I actually welcomed this exercise. Every detail of what had happened to me in the last few weeks was crystal clear in my beleaguered brain, and I wanted to share it with these people who might have some answers.

"Didn't the ER doctors order any tests or scans when you went there?" asked the leader of the group.

"No," I said, secretly hoping that the young Einstein who told me there was nothing wrong with my brain would get some sort of a demerit for it—maybe even be dismissed. I wasn't usually this vicious; it must have been the steroids they had just given me, which had miraculously cleared my double vision in a day.

"Mrs. Fricker, did you ever find yourself lost in familiar places in the weeks leading up to your first symptom?" asked another inquisitor. "Had any of your family members noticed a personality change in you?"

"No, I never got lost, and if my personality was different, no one ever mentioned it to me," I said. This game was getting old, and I needed to go back to bed.

At the end of the questioning, the head doctor asked me to imitate three things he did with his hand. He slapped the table open handed, then with the side of his hand, and then with his closed fist. In my head, I was frantically repeating, *Open, side, fist, open, side fist,* as if my ability to repeat his actions would win me a prize. I don't know if I did it right, but there was no prize.

After that, a nurse wheeled me into a waiting area while the doctors discussed my case, made their guesses, and then read the "answer sheet" of the pathology report to see how they scored.

The holding area I was in was a room filled with a group of brain-injured patients, many of whom were in wheelchairs wearing helmets. One woman, slumped to the side, kept repeating in a slow, slurred voice, "It's a beautiful morning," while a companion stroked her hair and said, "Yes, dear, it is a beautiful morning."

As disturbing as this scene was to me, I immediately fell asleep in my chair. I don't know how much time passed before I was tapped awake by a nurse. "There was 100 percent consensus among the group," she said with a smile. "They all agreed with the pathology report that you have large B-cell non-Hodgkin's lymphoma."

She looked at me expectantly at the end of her statement, as if awaiting a round of applause. All I could muster was, "Okay, thanks. Can I go back to bed now?"

At First They Flock

EVEN THOUGH I swiftly gave up on Googling my disease, the people in my life did not. They researched PCNSL right to the dire, doom-predicting end. The result? They turned out in droves to offer condolence, pep talks, pampering, and virtually anything and everything I wanted. (Note: When friends ask if there is anything they can do for you, never say no. Give them some small task, even if it's just picking up an iced coffee for you. They'll feel better.)

Al's brother, Guido, a quiet, nonsocial type of guy, arrived in my hospital room one morning with the first gift he had ever given me in thirty-two years. It was a book entitled *Crazy Sexy Cancer Survivor*, written by actress and author Kris Carr. Guido handed me the book and said, "Read it. This is good stuff, and don't worry, you're gonna be fine." As he left the room, he looked back at my bloated, steroid-ridden face and drooping eye and said with a smile, "See ya later, sexy."

The fact is that when you're first diagnosed with a catastrophic illness, your friends, family, and even casual acquaintances flock around you, both physically and emotionally. Phone calls never end, and visitors take a number in line as your hospital room bulges with well-wishers. And as sick as you feel, your mind is soothed by the cocoon of support that you think will always be there.

But the truth is, it probably won't be. As weeks and months go by, you're still fighting the battle of your life, but others slowly drift away and resume their normal routines. They have jobs and families, and the initial shock of losing their friend, colleague, or relative is over. They still call and send cards, but the huge posse of supporters gradually dwindles, and only a few stalwarts remain for the long haul. On an emotional level, I resented the mass departure, but logically, I understood it.

Lesson learned: When the flock disperses after your cancer diagnosis, don't panic. There is always someone to call—a neighbor who doesn't work, a retired relative, an American Cancer Society volunteer, or a local support group. You are never alone.

Panic and Self-Pity

My prescribed treatment plan for PCNSL was a biweekly regimen of high dose methotrexate—the chemotherapy drug of choice for this type of cancer—followed by a three-night stay in the hospital. The chemo had to be super tough to make its way through something called the "blood brain barrier" to get at my tumors. But it could also harm my internal organs, so after the infusion, the methotrexate would be flushed out of my system over several days, and I'd be given drugs to "rescue" my kidneys and other parts.

It was November 8, my daughter Alli's twenty-ninth birthday, and she spent it at the end of my hospital bed reading aloud from *People* magazine to take my mind off getting my first dose of this deadly toxin. Al was there, too, but he was pacing back and forth like a caged tiger, which really wasn't helping.

I was nervous, more afraid than I had been since the diagnosis. They were about to pour poison into my veins, and yet it was my only hope for survival. I had feared the word *chemotherapy* all my life, and now it was about to enter my body.

"This stuff is going to kill me," I said. "I'll be bald and dead before the cancer gets me."

"That's crazy," said Al, halting his pacing for a second. "I know lots of people who have had chemo, and they're doing great."

My fear on that night was off the charts, and looking back on it, I just wish that someone who had gotten chemo for any type of cancer could have talked with me before that first infusion went into my veins. If a survivor could have held my hand and said, "I had chemotherapy, and I'm still here," I would have felt so much less afraid.

As Alli started chattering about Kim Kardashian going on *Dancing with the Stars*, a sober-faced nurse entered, gowned from head to toe in blue paper. She was wheeling an IV pole that had a brown-covered bag suspended from it.

"I have to weigh and measure you before you get your infusion," she said. She helped me get on the scale and announced, "You are 156 centimeters and 151 pounds." She then hooked me up to an IV line that would pump the chemo through my system.

"I'm going to give you some Ativan to calm your nerves and something to prevent nausea, and then you can say good night to your visitors," she said.

I don't remember Al and Alli leaving, but I woke up the next morning to find that I was still alive.

Poland Sprung

"You can't get out of here until your methotrexate level is less than .2," said a perky young nurse named Christina. "So pee all you can to help us get rid of it."

I vowed to drink my way to freedom by overdosing on Poland Springs, and it worked. Wastebaskets overflowing with empty water bottles were a testament to the effort, and on the morning of the fourth day, I was told to pack my bags. I felt like hell, but round 1 was over, and I had survived.

When I got home that night, my niece Karen came over to remove my acrylic fingernails. Karen worked at a posh nail salon, and I had asked her to make a house call. I loved my fake nails with their cleverly named colors like Barefoot in Barcelona and Madison Mauvenue, but since I'd been sick, they had grown out and looked terrible. There was no way I would be able to keep up with them now, so I just wanted them gone.

I was lying facedown on the couch, too weak to turn my head, as chatty, blond-haired Karen went to work. She was my oldest niece, the daughter of Al's brother Guido and my best friend Sue, and I often joked with her that she and her two siblings owed me their lives because I had introduced her parents to each other on a blind date back in the seventies.

"Karen, I'm sorry I can't sit up for you to do this," I said. "I know it must be hard."

"Don't worry about a thing, Auntie Ree," she said cheerfully. "Just stick out your hand, and I'll do the rest."

She soaked my fingers in a bowl of alcohol that she had placed on the floor and gently peeled off each acrylic nail with the caution of dismantling a bomb. As she did her work, Karen described everything that was going on in an episode of *The Biggest Loser* that was playing on TV. I had not been able to concentrate on a television show since getting sick, but somehow her blow-by-blow description of this one (whose title seemed to mirror my current lot in life) piqued a glimmer of interest.

When my niece left, I looked at my real fingernails, which I hadn't seen in years. They were paper-thin with ugly yellow ridges on them, but I didn't care. Vanity, thy name is not cancer.

Treading Water

For the next two weeks, I vegetated at home, using a walker to get around and alternating between staring blankly at a wall and complaining about my symptoms to anyone who would listen, including my poor dog Otis, a fourteen-year-old blind and arthritic pug who must have been longing for euthanasia. I knew I was being a total drag on everyone around me, and sometimes I felt bad about that, but mostly I was just too sick to care.

My life with cancer was so drastically different from the existence I had led before the two white spots had invaded my brain. I had always been the organizer, the one who got others together, made plans for dinner, and filled every waking moment with someplace to go and something to do. An occasional unscheduled Saturday night at home was breeding grounds for anxiety, although Al appreciated being able to sit in front of the TV and eat his pork rinds on those rare occasions. Now there were no plans to be made, no work to be done—just the challenge of staying alive until tomorrow. And that was more than enough diversion.

Al Fricker—a Survivor

My husband Al has never been diagnosed with a life-threatening disease, but if he were, I know he would survive. His life is a carefully scheduled routine from which he never wavers. He works six days a week driving a truck for a big supermarket as he has done for the last thirty-five years.

Sunday is Al's only day off, and he has every moment of it planned for particular pursuits—most of which take place in the basement of our house. He makes out bills, does laundry, dusts his hundreds of model cars, drops the trash off at the town dump, and drinks beer while leaning back in an office chair listening to loud music.

My brain tumor was not part of Al Fricker's neatly ordered routine. At first, he was completely in denial, believing that this disastrous turn of events had never really occurred. Then when he realized it was true, Al decided that he could continue his normal sixty-hour work schedule, and I would be all right with the help of others in my life.

One Sunday morning, while I was at home recuperating from my first chemo treatment, Alli and I were sitting at the kitchen table, and Al was in the cellar involved in his usual self-assigned activities. I yelled down to ask him if he would wash a load of pajamas for me. My earlier requests that day had included bringing me bottles of water, feeding the dog, and figuring out the TV remote a couple of times. Each of these duties had required him to stop what he was doing, ascend from the cellar, and set his schedule off for the amount of time it took to complete the task. Hence, my final request for him to do a load of laundry put him right over the edge.

He came up the stairs looking like Mr. Bluster, a character on the fifties-era *Howdy Doody* show who was always blowing off steam. His parents had given him this nickname when he would throw temper tantrums as a child.

"Is there anything else you need from me?" he shouted. "I have things to do. I work sixty hours a week, and this is my only day off."

I was incredibly hurt by what he was saying, but also angry. "You know something Al, I'm sick, and you just might have to alter your schedule for a while to help me out."

His eyes narrowed into thin blue slits as he said, "Then I'd rather be dead."

For the first time since my diagnosis, I put my head on the table and cried—heaving, shoulder-shaking sobs as I thought of the total trap I was in of being dependent on others for my daily needs. I had always been a strong, self-sufficient person, and now I was completely vulnerable and needy.

Alli got up from the table and attacked her father with a stream of vitriol that seemed to go on forever. "How dare you talk to Mom like that?" she said. "She's the one who matters now, not your foolish schedule. It's time for you to start stepping up to the plate, Dad. Nobody gives a damn about your only day off."

At the end of this chastisement, Al was in tears, which I had only witnessed once before, on the day after his mother died when he realized that he hadn't told her he loved her.

"I'm so sorry, Ree. I didn't mean it," he said. "I should never have said that. I didn't mean it. I'll do anything you want."

He pulled a chair up between Alli and me at the table and put his arms around us both.

From that day forward, Al changed—not a lot, but enough. He still spent most of his Sundays doing his own thing in the basement, but he was there for me every night, telling me he loved me and that I was going to be okay. "You're going to be better than ever," he'd say, tapping me on the head. "You're not leaving me."

My baldness didn't seem to bother him, nor did my twenty-pound weight gain, which resulted from prolonged steroid treatment. He never made me feel ashamed of this "new" and not improved me. Even when I told him about people not recognizing me on the street, he said, "Don't worry about that, Ree. It's just the short hair."

Lesson learned: If your spouse or partner is your soul mate and is with you every step of the way in your cancer journey, count your blessings. If not or if you're single, try to have a network of people who can fill the gap. Keep your friends. You'll know who they are when the flock disperses.

It's a Jungle in Here

WHEN JAY MOVED out of the house after college, I had converted his old room into an African safari-themed guest room. It was crazy, but I got the idea after touring Elvis Presley's Tennessee mansion with my sister years before. The *Graceland* estate, which was modest by today's celebrity standards, had an incredible jungle room in the lower level, with animal skins, leopard pillows, zebra lamps, lions' heads, and at least twenty TVs on the walls. I loved it and decided to create a poor man's version of it in my own little 1,400 square-foot Garrison.

I selected lifelike replicas of jungle animals—a five-foot-tall metal giraffe, a stuffed tiger, a brass monkey holding up a "leaf" table like a serving dish, and photographs of elephants on the Serengeti. I even ordered a piece of abstract artwork that was painted by Cheetah, the chimpanzee from the early Tarzan movies.

"Are you out of your mind?" my coworker Nancy said when I told her about the $135 purchase of the famous chimp's painting. "You're crazy. How do you know the monkey even painted it?"

"How do I know? Just check out this certificate of authenticity," I said, unrolling a parchment scroll that had come with the painting. "Don't you see his black thumbprint at the bottom? That's his official signature."

At that point everyone was in hysterics.

"Go ahead and laugh," I said. "You guys are just jealous. Cheetah is seventy years old and living in a California primate sanctuary. Do you people realize that this chimp once held the hand of Johnny Weissmuller?"

"Who's that?" said my staff in unison. All of them were too young to remember the actor and former Olympic swimmer who had played Tarzan when I was a child.

I didn't know it then, but the jungle room was to become my sanctuary in the battle of my life. Al has always been a huge snorer and is quite difficult to sleep with, even in a king-sized bed. Hence, on more nights than not, I would grab my pillow and shuffle into the jungle room, where I found blissful silence. After a while, I slept there on most nights instead of making the nocturnal trips across the hall.

But when I was diagnosed with the brain tumor, stricken with fear, I returned to the master bedroom, thinking I could somehow find protection lying next to my 220-pound husband. I quickly realized, however, that Al's presence couldn't help me, that he still snored, and that he still got up at 3:30 a.m. to head for work.

Each morning as his alarm went off, I would bolt upright and remain awake for an even longer day of coping with symptoms and anxieties. So I soon moved back into the comforting surrounds of my jungle room, and that's where I recuperated for the next year.

Al didn't seem to mind the abandonment. In fact, I think he was glad to put some space between him and this whimpering, clinging creature that had replaced his previously feisty and independent wife. And who knows, maybe in the back of his slightly neurotic mind he was thinking, *Could I catch this from her?*

Hair It Goes

WHEN DR. NORDEN had explained the type of chemo I would be receiving after the diagnosis, the first thing I had asked was, "Will I go bald?"

"I don't think so," he'd said. "Methotrexate doesn't usually cause much hair loss."

Once again, add me to the minority. As I was blow-drying my hair in the bathroom a few weeks after my first treatment, I was horrified to see the white sink filling up with chunks of brown hair. It was coming out in fistfuls.

"My hair is falling out," I yelled down the stairs to Al. "Come quick and do something." My mother's three-word plea to my father whenever there was a crisis in the house—an invading mouse or bird, a pan fire, or a skunk-sprayed pet—was always, "Henry, do something!" I guess I had inherited her damsel-in-distress behavior.

Al ran up the stairs and looked at the hair-filled sink. "It's okay, Ree," he said. "We knew this might happen. There's no reason to panic. You can get a wig."

I had always liked my hair, which was thick and wavy and had stayed brown long after my peers had gone gray. Losing it bothered me. It made me look sick. It made me look like what I was—a cancer patient—and I hated it.

It turned out that Dr. Norden had been partially right. I never went totally bald from the methotrexate, so I was glad I didn't get the buzz-cut that my friend Elaine had suggested, but I did have big empty patches on my scalp. My health insurance covered the cost of a wig, so Betty, Jay, and I went to the Friends Boutique at Dana-Farber one afternoon in December to pick out my new look.

"Here, try this one," said Betty, handing me a purple Mohawk for a laugh. "Yeah, that's definitely you."

After trying on everything, from Shirley Temple curls to flowing blond tresses, I found a Raquel Welch wig, which was almost identical to my own hairstyle and color.

"I love that one," said Jay. "It will make you look better than you ever looked with your own hair."

"Thanks a lot."

Like Mrs. Brady of *Brady Bunch* fame, I've had the same hairdo (a shoulder-length angle cut) for most of my adult life. I had often brought magazine pictures of desired new looks to my hairdresser only to have her say, "But this is the hairstyle you already have."

"It is?" I'd say with genuine surprise. "No wonder I liked it."

I took my sister's advice and bought the Raquel Welch wig because it looked the most like the old me. I wanted to be the same person I was before the cancer diagnosis in so many ways, and at least this helped a little.

My Son, My Savior

WHEN IT WAS time for my second chemo treatment, Jay arrived at the house early and drove me to the hospital in a ritual that would become our routine for the next thirteen months. He brought me to the Dana-Farber infusion lab, sat with me while I got the chemo, and then waited for hours staring down at his iPhone until an oncology room became available so that I could be admitted.

I'm sure the medical staff must have wondered where my husband was, but Al's salary was all we had supporting us now, and he didn't have the sick or vacation time to help me out. To be honest, even if he did, I would have chosen Jay as my go-to person in this crisis anyway. Al and I love each other, but we are not the attached-at-the hip couple that many spouses are. Besides, I would have had to worry about him getting antsy from having to wait around for so long at the hospital.

"We have a room for you now," said a young dark-haired nurse, smiling at my son, who returned the grin. Jay hauled my pillow, comforter, and suitcase behind him while the nurse pushed my wheelchair onto an elevator and got me settled in a room on the fifth floor oncology unit. "Oh look, Ma," he said. "You've got the side with the window this month."

"Nice," I said, feigning some enthusiasm. "Do you have to leave now, Jay?"

"Yeah, I've gotta go to work," he said, hanging my pink bathrobe on a chair beside my bed and heading for the door. "You're gonna be fine. Call me if you need anything."

"You are the best son in the world," I said. "I hope you know that."

"Yeah, right," he said flashing his one-dimple grin. You like Alli better."

The Lowest Ebb

AFTER JAY LEFT, I fell asleep early as I had during the first treatment. But this time, I woke up hours later with terrible stomach pains and an awful tightness in my jaw.

I dragged my IV pole to the bathroom and looked in the mirror. What stared back at me was a monstrous swollen face with red balloon eyes that were nearly fused shut. I was also shaking and having terrible cramps. I thought about the year of chemo treatments that lay ahead of me and knew it was impossible. I would never be able to endure them.

I sat down on the floor next to the toilet, doubled over and crying, trying to hold my IV pole with one hand so it wouldn't fall over. As I look back on this moment now, this was probably the lowest ebb of my journey. Eventually, a nurse pried me out of the bathroom and sent for the on-call doctor.

"You need to calm down, Mrs. Fricker," he said. "You're probably just bloated from the steroids. I'm going to give you some Benadryl, and you should try to get some rest."

I didn't believe him. I had been on steroids for weeks, and my face never looked like this.

When Dr. Norden came by the next morning, I was sitting in bed staring at an untouched bowl of oatmeal on my breakfast tray. "What the heck happened to you?" he said, coming closer to my bloated face.

"I was hoping you could tell me," I said, dabbing my sore, slit eyes with a Kleenex.

"Okay, don't worry, Marie. You've had an allergic reaction to one of the drugs. It's probably the methotrexate, which means we'll have to give you the next treatments in the ICU until we can desensitize you to it. It's a little more complicated but doable. The only other medication you got was Zofran, an antinausea drug, and I've never heard of anyone being allergic to that. I'll set up an appointment with an allergist right away to find out what's going on."

ICUs, complications. Could this get any worse?

"Don't worry," said Dr. Norden, patting my shoulder. "We'll figure this out."

Al came over that night and stayed until nine thirty, long past visiting hours. He brought a blue rubber ice pack, which helped with the swelling on my face. Billy also stopped by with a pair of size XL men's boxer shorts that I had asked him to buy since I had become a bloated tic and could no longer fit into any of my clothes.

A few days later, I met with an allergy doctor in the ICU at the Brigham. He injected my hand with a tiny needle containing methotrexate and waited. Nothing happened. Then he shot in some Zofran. Within minutes, a red bubble popped up on my hand, and my neck flushed red.

"Wow, this is very unusual, but you're in luck," he said with a smile. "You are allergic to your antinausea drug, not to your chemotherapy."

I didn't feel very lucky, but I'd take it. There was always Pepto-Bismol.

The Polar Bear Cometh

AFTER SPENDING TWO weeks at home recovering from the last treatment, it was time to line up my ride into the hospital for the next one. Jay was working, and nobody else I called was available to take me in. At this point, I was never more than seconds away from panic, and this put it into overdrive.

What if no one can take me for my chemo treatment? What if this happens a lot? How will I get better? Everyone has forgotten about me now. What if I'm stuck in my house for weeks on end, never seeing a friendly face? Looking back on it now, I was totally overreacting, but at that time, there were some valid reasons to fear not being able to get to the hospital every month. Al was still working his six-day week, and my sister, who had recently retired from a forty-three-year career with Verizon, had taken a job at Macy's and was also substitute teaching. Jay was unreachable during his two twenty-four-hour shifts as a firefighter, and Alli had gone back to teaching a classroom of second graders after her maternity leave was over. Everyone else I knew had full-time jobs.

In a wave of self-pity, I realized that I was no longer a viable member of society. I was not the award-winning Cecilia B. DeFricker. I was useless and unproductive, and like an elderly Eskimo woman, I might as well be put out onto an iceberg for a polar bear to eat. (Google it—they did that.)

Dissolving into tears, I assumed my go-to fetal position on the couch as somebody on TV said, "Congratulations, you've won the big deal of the day."

When Al came up from the cellar, he said. "What's wrong, Ree? Are you in pain?"

I turned around to look at him. "No one can take me for my chemo on Friday. I've asked everyone. What am I going to do? What if this happens every month?"

Al knelt on the floor next to the sofa and took my face in his rough truck driver hands. "I know I haven't been as involved in all this as you think I should be," he said. "But if I don't go to work, we won't have any money with the loss of your paycheck. [This really wasn't helping me.] But I swear you will never miss a single chemotherapy treatment or a single doctor's appointment. If nobody else can take you, I will."

I couldn't help wondering why I needed to exhaust all other resources before my own husband would step up to the plate, but I was too weak to question it. For now, I accepted the terms and felt better.

Giving Thanks — Sort Of

THANKSGIVING WAS ALWAYS a big holiday for me because it was the only one that I hosted at my house. Al would bitch and moan about all the work it entailed, but at the end of the day, he was always glad we did it. This year, however, just a few weeks into chemo treatment and feeling hopeless, I had no interest in it.

But Jay was having none of that. "We have Thanksgiving at our house every year, and we're going to have it here this year too," he said. "I will order the food from the Silent Chef, and Alli and I will serve the dinner. Nothing's changed."

Was he serious? Everything had changed. On Thanksgiving morning, I was lying on the sofa in a nightgown as Jay ran around heating up side dishes, carving the turkey, and putting our Thanksgiving decorations and centerpiece on the table. This kid was something else. He had always seemed so bored at these annual dinners, but I guess they really meant a lot to him.

"Mom, you are not coming to the table dressed like that," he said, pouring gravy into a turkey-shaped bowl. "You need to go upstairs and put something else on."

Reluctantly, I did what he said and came down in a new beige velour sweat suit with a white fur collar that someone had bought me for the hospital.

"That's better," said Jay. "By the way, Aunt Chris isn't coming. She has a virus, and her doctor didn't want her spreading germs to someone who's getting chemotherapy."

Chris was my brother-in-law Bill's sister and a good friend, and she always joined us for the holidays. This was the first Thanksgiving in thirty-two years that she wouldn't be with us, and I felt bad about that. But since starting the chemo, I lived in fear of other people's coughs and sneezes and truly believed that catching the common cold would kill me.

When the relatives arrived, I pushed myself to the dinner table in an office chair on wheels. I ate ravenously, as was my new steroid-driven MO, and spoke very little. In fact, the only comment I can remember was, "Pass the mashed potatoes, please."

My voracious appetite seemed to fill some sort of basic, almost primordial need when nothing else mattered. The idea of socializing with my loved ones on what might be my last Thanksgiving with them wasn't even on my radar. I was operating almost entirely on animal instinct in the early months of my illness—eating, sleeping, and staring vacantly into space.

I Did It on a Lark

I WAS A few months into treatment and feeling weaker than an abandoned baby squirrel when Alli insisted on taking me with her to the supermarket on a Saturday morning. When we got there, she told me to use one of the "Lark" motorized scooters for disabled customers and do my own shopping.

"Are you kidding me," I said. "There is no way I'm getting into that thing. Are you trying to make me feel worse about myself?"

"Okay, then you're going to have to push a carriage and walk through the store."

I recognized the tough love tactic she was using, so I sat down stubbornly on a bench, figuring she would relent and walk me back to the car. Instead, she grabbed a cart and disappeared into the produce section of the market.

I thought about the huge store and my wobbly legs and decided to throw pride out the window. I hoisted myself into the Lark and started navigating the aisles, picking items off the lower shelves and putting them into the basket. I was amazed that I could actually maneuver this thing, but I also had an urgent need to explain my use of it to other shoppers.

And that was exactly what I did—over and over again to anyone who had the misfortune of looking my way. "A few months ago, I was a normal person, and then I got this burning hot foot, and eight days later, I was in a wheelchair with a brain tumor."

People would gasp in amazement as I ended my story by pointing at my head (to indicate the location of the brain, I guess.) I'm sure they wanted to escape this sad, slumped woman in the scooter, but they dutifully heard me out and sympathized accordingly.

Alli told me later that she was mortified whenever she entered a new aisle and saw me talking to another stranger and pointing to my head.

"You Like Me,
You Really Like Me!"

—Sally Field, Dolby Theater, 1984

THE JACK CONWAY Company has an internal newsletter called the *Gram*, which is published by our ad department. Shortly after my hospitalization, someone from work e-mailed me "A Special Conway Get Well Gram."

It had my photo on it, and our CEO had written, "As many of you know, our much loved advertising director has been diagnosed with a rare, but treatable form of cancer (Of course it has to be rare, Marie Fricker is anything but typical.) Marie is a favorite of all of us with her high energy and cheerful spirit, and I'm asking all of you to send her a card to let her know you're thinking of her."

The get-well cards arrived en masse—hundreds of them— and I appreciated it. Of course, as I started to get better and my cynical side reemerged, I began keeping track of the people at work who hadn't sent me a card and actually made a "What the hell?" list of their names.

My need to be liked and accepted by my peers began as a young child growing up with a "don't bug me" teenage sister and two older parents. My mother was thirty-eight when I was born and my father forty-four. The houses on both sides of mine had families of seven and eight children, and I wanted so much to live in one of them. At night, when our outdoor games of hide-and-seek were finished, my friends would go home and continue playing inside with their siblings while I was relegated to watching TV with two adults who had no desire to seek me if I hid.

"I'm hiding," I'd yell to my mother from the bedroom. "Come and find me."

"Yeah, Ree Ree, I'll be right there," she'd say. After a while, I'd come out of my spot only to find her dozing over a book with her eyeglasses slipping off her nose.

As I got older, my desire to be liked continued to the point where I was willing to be a lackey for the "cool kids" in high school who were more than eager to cheat off my test papers but not so eager to ask me to hang out.

So here I was at age 55, like Sally Field accepting her Oscar for *Norma Rae*, counting hundreds of get-well cards and thinking, *They like me, they really like me,* and worrying about the ones who didn't.

Don't Move Your Head

A FEW DAYS after one of my early chemo treatments, I took the hospital elevator down to the MRI suite and made out the paperwork to enter the black tunnel of anything but love for yet another scan. The questions on the pretest form went on forever:

Do you have a wire mesh implant?

Do you have a cardiac pacemaker?

Do you have any body piercings, stents, or shunts?

I guess they didn't want some metal object trying to escape my body and gluing me to the scanner.

I made Xs in dozens of yes or no boxes on the form and handed it back to the receptionist. Looking through the glass door to the hallway outside, I could see the Jimmy Fund Red Sox baseball murals lining the lobby walls. Other patients were flipping through magazines and staring at cell phones while they waited to be called.

My head was woozy from taking a Xanax that morning to ward off the claustrophobia that always hit me during the forty-five minutes of solitary confinement. But now my eyes were starting to close, and I could barely stay awake. Maybe

I was actually getting used to this procedure and didn't need the tranquilizer any more.

Falling asleep is absolutely forbidden inside the MRI tube because people involuntarily move their heads during sleep. I found that out the hard way a month ago when a burly nurse hauled me out of the machine when I had drifted off from utter exhaustion during a middle-of-the-night scan.

"I'm going to have to take these pictures all over again," she said angrily. "You were moving your head all over the place."

This woman obviously wasn't enjoying her graveyard shift at the hospital, and I fully expected the next words out of her mouth to be, "What the f—— is wrong with you?"

I decided to go cold turkey for the next MRI; no more Xanax.

Musings from Infusings

I HAD BEEN keeping a written journal since the start of my illness after reading in some of my "coping with cancer" books that it was a good thing to do. I mentioned to my nephew Billy that on some days I was just too weak to write, so he bought me a tiny pocket tape recorder to use. I did a lot of dictating while waiting for chemo treatments in the Dana-Farber infusion lab. It passed the time and seemed to lessen the bleakness of the surroundings.

Here's my first dictated journal entry:

> I'm in here for another treatment while Jay sits across from me in a high-backed visitor's chair, staring into his iPhone. He is wearing a Red Sox baseball cap, a white polo shirt, jean shorts and new white Nikes—appropriate "good guy" attire for this incredibly good guy. On his right calf, a tattoo of a bulldog's head he'd gotten at eighteen is staring at me with its grinning snarl. I told him he would regret that accessory someday, and at twenty-six, he already does.
>
> My chemo nurse is Mary Clancy, a heavyset woman in her late forties with a short brown hairdo and a no-nonsense attitude, but her eyes belie her manner. She is kind. Cancer patients are sitting in

blue leather recliners throughout the room with IVs hooked up to them. Little TV monitors are mounted high on the walls, but no one seems to look at them.

A dark-haired woman is reading a book next to a young man whose head is shaved on one side, showing a big jagged scar. She is wearing silver hoop earrings and a puffy pink jacket with high-laced boots. A man in a khaki work shirt is leaning back on a pillow while his wife thumbs through the pages of *Glamour* magazine. She has a Dunkin' Donuts coffee on the tray beside her—a symbol of normalcy in this abnormal world.

A cheerful old guy with a bow tie offers me a sandwich and snacks from a pushcart. "Hey, honey, what looks good to you?" he asks. "How about a nice tuna on rye? I've got some Doritos here too."

Mary asked me to give her another urine sample. "Your PH level has to come up before I can start your chemo," she said.

I had no idea what that meant, but I dutifully trudged off to the bathroom, pushing my pole in front of me. It is time to do anything and everything they tell me to—not bravery, just desperation.

The question is, how in God's name did I end up in this strange and exclusive new club? I know I never applied for membership, but I sure am paying the dues.

Chemo Brain—It's for Real

FOR A COUPLE of weeks, I invented a new game while sitting in the "pre-infusion" waiting area at the Dana. I tried to guess which person out of each couple in the room was the cancer patient and which was the companion.

I would check out each one's demeanor, smiling or solemn; hair, sparse or healthy looking; skin tone, pale or pink. And then I'd identify the cancer patient. Sometimes it was easy, and sometimes I was wrong.

I did this for almost a month before I realized that the cancer patient within each pair was quite obviously wearing a white hospital ID bracelet on one wrist. Would I have detected this clue earlier if I didn't have chemo brain?

Journal entry:

My nurse's aide today is Karleen, and she's from St. Lucia. She's wearing a bright yellow smock with blue and red sailboats on it, and she smells like lavender soap. She greets me every morning with a cheerful, "Hello, girlfriend. How are you today?" She has shoulder-length black hair, gold hoop earrings, and something amazing—my mother's smile. I thought I might be imagining it at first, so I introduced her to Betty one day, and she couldn't believe the resemblance. I told Karleen that if I ever get better, she and I are going to dinner.

The on-call medical team just left after the daily check-in. Today it was Dr. Wasell and her physician's assistants, Jen and Janice. When I get the PAs alone, I will have to ask them about PCNSL and my chances for survival. They are always more willing to talk than the doctors and much more upbeat.

Too Old to Have a Roommate

NEVER HAVING BEEN an inpatient in a hospital before except to give birth, I had not considered the issue of cohabiting with another person in a trapped state of existence. But the obvious fact is that everyone on the oncology floors at Brigham and Women's Hospital has cancer, so the thought of rooming with a pleasant tonsillectomy patient or an entertaining narcissist just in for a tummy tuck was not on the agenda.

Occupying a semiprivate room means that you are sharing a space and a bathroom with a stranger who may be crying continuously, staring at you when you aren't expecting it, ripping out IVs, or ringing nurse's help bells at all hours of the night.

Although they came and went rapidly during my inpatient stays at the Brigham over a thirteen-month period, four of my roommates left a lasting impression.

Mary

Mary was an eighty-seven-year-old librarian from Arlington, which was my original hometown, but we had something more in common—our very rare disease. She too had been diagnosed with PCNSL and was a patient of Dr. Andrew

Norden. She, however, was dealing with her cancer much better than I was.

"I am not afraid at all," said Mary. "I really think I'm going to beat this thing. And if I don't, well, I'm eighty-seven, and I've had a great life."

Her optimism was nice, but it wasn't contagious. Mary was smart and funny. She had moved to Arlington in 1954, the year after I was born, and being with her made me feel at home. One night, when neither of us had any visitors due to a howling snowstorm making the windows in our room opaque, we watched *Jeopardy* together, each calling out answers and getting a lot of them right, despite our mutual chemo brains.

I had a rare feeling of well-being when the show was over and the old *Wizard of Oz* movie came on TV. I fell asleep to the tune of "We're Off to See the Wizard." If only the wizard could solve this problem, it would be "To Oz or bust!"

The next month, I asked Dr. Norden to pull some strings so that Mary and I could share a room again. "Well, since you two are my favorite patients, I'll see what I can do," he said. He came through, and while Mary and I waited for our breakfast trays, we talked about having a reunion at a steak house in Arlington when we both felt better.

"Arlington isn't a dry town anymore, you know," she said. "So I'll buy us a bottle of champagne, and you bring some old photo albums from when you lived there. We'll have a great time."

I looked for Mary the next month and the month after that but never saw her around. When I questioned Dr. Norden about her, he seemed evasive. "Why do you keep asking me about Mary?" he said one morning with an irritated tone, which was unlike him. Was it some kind of patient-doctor confidentiality thing that was bothering him?

"I was just wondering where she is," I said.

"Well, I'll tell you then. Mary died last week."

"Oh my god."

"Now remember, Marie, she had your illness, but she was eighty-seven years old," he said. "Don't compare your two cases."

I was sad for Mary and terrified for me.

Jesus Save Me—from Diana

Diana was a glamorous-looking woman in her early forties with an unidentified form of cancer, meaning she wouldn't tell me what it was. She spent a lot of time brushing her long brown hair and talking about Jesus. She was a born-again Christian and was sure she would be cured.

"I know the Lord will hear my prayers, Marie, and He will save you too," she said. "You just have to admit you're a sinner. We are all sinners, and Jesus will save you if you repent for your sins and recognize him as your Lord and Savior."

Diana was a nonstop talker, and I had to pretend to be asleep to avoid her constant banter. One afternoon, I got up from my bed, pushing my IV pole ahead of me to get to the bathroom, which was on her side of the room. When I pulled back the curtain between us, she was standing at the sink removing her wig. Her head was bald except for a few long strands of brown hair still clinging to the surface.

She saw me and launched into a full-blown verbal attack. "Why are you staring at me?" she yelled. "I didn't want you to see my hair. You did that on purpose."

"I didn't even know you were wearing a wig," I said. "I was just trying to get to the bathroom. My own hair is falling out. What would I care about yours?"

"Just leave me alone," she said, closing the green-and-white checked curtain between us with a dramatic sweep. "I don't want you to look at me."

The rest of our interactions during bathroom trips were stiff and awkward, but there was an upside to the situation. She no longer cared about saving my soul. I heaved a sigh of relief when Diana was discharged and replaced by a woman who never spoke a word.

A Is for Alice

I guess I must like librarians or the elderly because another roommate who proved to be a gem was a ninety-one-year-old library worker from the North Shore of Boston. Her name was Alice, and she had been battling leukemia quietly for the last five years. As I was wheeled past her bed to mine on the day I met her, she was wearing a blue linen dress, sitting in a chair, and munching on a ham-and-cheese sandwich and a bag of chips. She gave a friendly wave and continued eating.

As we got to know each other during our weekend at the hospital, I asked Alice to tell me the key to living into her nineties. "Well, I never ate a vegetable in my life," she said. "I had a couple of martinis a day, and I smoked for twenty years. I truly think that longevity is in your genes."

Not good news for me whose parents had died at sixty-nine and seventy-one.

"I had a grandfather who lived ten days beyond his one hundredth birthday, and he drank like a fish."

The vestiges of great beauty were in Alice's face, and although she never married or had children, she had close relationships with her nieces and nephews, a few of whom visited her regularly. She walked around our room in white

Rockport sneakers and had a quick laugh and an upbeat attitude. I liked her. Her roommate rating was an A.

Sarah

Sarah was a pretty, fit-looking woman in her early forties with blonde, peach-fuzz hair that was just growing in after chemo. She had been diagnosed with multiple myeloma nine years earlier but had gone into remission until a recent recurrence, and she was sure she was dying. She cried loud bawling sobs all day long, and if she was awakened in the wee hours of the morning for a blood pressure check or any other reason, the wailing began again. She had a sweet husband, Ken, who often brought us both treats from the hospital deli, and a pretty twelve-year-old daughter, Jessica, whom she adored.

During one of Sarah's extended crying spells in the middle of the night, I heard her calling my name. "Marie, can you please come sit with me?" she said, choking back sobs. "I'm so afraid."

"I'll be right there," I said, not sure that I could make it to her side of the room with my trail of tubes and wires. Pushing my IV pole ahead of me, I slid back the curtain that separated us and sat on the edge of her bed. She put her hand out, and I held it. Her eyes were puffy and her skin red and blotchy from weeping, but she looked a little relieved. For the first time since my illness, I was the caregiver, the person who was comforting someone else, and it felt good.

"You're just scared, Sarah. It's going to be all right," I said. "I'm scared too, but we're both in the best place in the world to treat what's wrong with us. You have so much to live for, and you're gonna make it."

My roommate held tightly to my hand, and by the end of our talk, she was making nasty but very funny comments about one of our male nurses. "I think Luke has a thing for me, and I don't appreciate it," she said. "I am totally capable of going to the bathroom without his assistance, and I've told him that on multiple occasions, and yet he still keeps asking, 'Do you need any help in there?'" We laughed like schoolgirls sharing a secret.

When Sarah was discharged, we exchanged phone numbers, and a few months later, I tried to reach her at home. I left several voice mail messages, but no one ever called me back. Eventually, I got up the nerve to Google her name and saw what I was petrified to see. The obituary ended with, "She leaves behind her husband Kenneth and twelve-year-old daughter Jessica." I cried until my eyes were as puffy as Sarah's had been on the night we held hands. I resolved to never again become emotionally attached to another roommate. And, selfishly, I never did.

Journal entry:

I'm back in the hospital for another spa treatment. I got up at 6:00 a.m. Well, not "up" since I am still lying down. My new roommate is a bit of an exhibitionist, so I'm planning to keep the curtain between us closed at all times.

On the wall in front of me is a TV/VCR unit and a whiteboard bearing the news, "Today is Friday, November 21, 2008. Your RN's name is Kim. Your personal care attendant's name is Evelyn. Have a great day."

Yeah, like that's gonna happen.

Any Port in a Storm

I HAD BEEN having chemo treatments for several months, and each time, my veins would balk at the intrusion of the IV needles, leaving me black and blue from elbow to wrist. Dr. Norden made the decision to fit me with a PowerPort, a portable catheter that would be inserted into my chest, just under the skin.

"The procedure is done under conscious sedation and only takes about thirty minutes," he said. "Trust me, Marie, you'll be so glad you had it done. It will give you quick and painless access for all of your chemotherapy and IV meds from now on. You'll love it."

The day came for the surgery, and I was scared. My sister walked beside me as I was wheeled on a gurney to the pre-op area. I'd had nothing to eat or drink that morning, and I could hear my stomach churning. Tears were slipping out of my eyes onto the pillowcase under my head.

"What are you crying about?" said an older nurse with gray hair and piercing blue eyes. "This is nothing. Not even as bad as getting a filling."

An aide with a strong Jamaican accent came over and kneeled next to my stretcher. "What's wrong, honey?" she asked.

"I'm scared," I said, and with that, my sister started crying too.

"Oh, this doesn't hurt at all, and you will be so happy you had it done. God is with you, and you will be fine."

Her words made me feel a little better as I was wheeled into the operating room. I was given a Versed drip through an IV, and the fear disintegrated. I felt a steady pressure just under my clavicle as the surgeon, a young Asian woman, hovered above me, pushing and pressing, but there was no pain. During the procedure, someone was holding my hand and stroking my right thumb the whole time, which was so comforting. And in no time, a nurse was telling me that it was over.

"You're done, sweetie," she said. "Your port is all set to use on your next chemo treatment. You did great."

"Thanks, it really wasn't that bad," I said. "I shouldn't have been such a wimp. Would you please thank whoever was holding my hand during the procedure? That helped me so much."

The nurse looked at me oddly and said, "Mrs. Fricker, there was no one holding your hand."

I know she was wrong.

Rain on My Parade

AFTER MY SECOND chemo treatment, Dr. Norden ordered another MRI to check on the status of my tumors. He came into my hospital room the next morning looking pumped. "I'm very pleased," he said. "Both lesions are shrinking. Your lymphoma is no match for my methotrexate."

My heart raced as I dared for a minute to believe him. I grabbed a piece of paper and wrote down his last statement, "Your lymphoma is no match for my methotrexate." I put it in my pocketbook for future reference.

While I was reveling in the good news from the MRI, a muscular guy in blue scrubs walked in and introduced himself as Victor, my day nurse. After talking with him for a while, he told me he was a Hodgkin's lymphoma survivor and that he had frozen his stem cells ten years ago in case he ever needed a transplant.

"Wow, that's great that you are a survivor," I said, secretly annoyed that his Hodgkin's variety of lymphoma was highly curable and mine was not. "So what do you know about my disease? Does the treatment I'm getting usually work well?"

"Sometimes," he said. "But even if it doesn't, you have two to three years ahead of you. There's nothing immediate to fear here. It's not like you're going to die tomorrow. You'll have two more Christmases, two more birthdays."

A chill ran down my spine. Two years? My grandson won't even remember me. I reached into my purse for the quote from Dr. Norden and read it twice. It wasn't helping.

"Would you like some graham crackers, Mrs. Fricker?" Victor asked, putting a package on my nightstand.

"No, thank you," I said, turning away from him. "I need to sleep now."

A month ago, I'd had a lifetime to look forward to and now…two birthdays. I wanted to say, "Thanks a lot, Victor, for ruining what could have been my first hopeful day," but I said nothing as he took back his crackers and left.

Send in the Shrinks

WHEN YOU ARE a patient at the Brigham, you get the benefits of a teaching hospital with a staff that treats the "whole person," not just the sick person. Your religious needs are met by chaplains and priests, your rehab needs are met by social workers and physical therapists, and your psychological needs are met by an in-house team of mental health professionals.

I met the head psychiatrist, Dr. Vito, one morning while playing Scrabble on my laptop. She was a tall, impeccably-dressed woman in her fifties with wire-framed glasses that sat low on her nose. She introduced herself and the three students who were following her and asked me some questions about my state of mind before the illness struck.

"Were you anxious or depressed before you became ill?" she asked, peering at me over her glasses. "Have you ever been in therapy?"

"Well, I've always been a nervous person," I said. "But not depressed. In fact, I had a great life before all this started. I have never seen a therapist, but I would gladly welcome one now."

"Are you able to deal with your anxiety?" she asked. "Dr. Norden tells me that you're very afraid."

"I have been told that I have brain cancer, and I don't want to die. Yes, I'm very afraid, and no, I'm not dealing with it well. Sometimes I wake up in the night in sheer panic and feel like I can't breathe." At this point I was crying, and she handed me a tissue.

After a few more questions, she and her entourage left to study my case. They came back the next day with a prescription for clonazepam. "I'd like you to try this," she said. "It's an antianxiety agent that stays in your system longer than Xanax, and it doesn't have the letdown effect. It will help to keep you on an even keel during what you're going through."

"Hey, you had me at 'Try this,'" I said. I was not a martyr, and I wanted anything that could help me cope with the nightmare I was living. Apparently, the psychiatric team had decided that I was relatively normal, and I didn't see much of them after that.

However, from time to time, Dr. V. would pop in to give me some little mental games to play.

"Now, Mrs. Fricker, I'm going to say three words—*brown*, *tulips*, and *honesty*—and I want you to repeat them back to me at the end of our session." Then she would ask me to draw a clock on some paper and set it for 11:20 and copy some geometric shapes that she had drawn. At the end of the exercise, I would say, "Brown, honesty, and tulips," and she would give me my score, which was always 100 percent.

Great," she would say. "Now let's compare that score to your test results when you were first diagnosed and see how far you've come." She would then flip through her notes and say, "Oh, you got 100 then too." I was lucky that my tumors had not been located in a cognitive part of my brain, so even though my head felt like it was wrapped in twenty pounds of gauze, I had always been able to think.

"Dr. Vito, I have something to tell you," I said after one of our bedside tests. "You always give me the same three words to memorize—*tulips*, *brown*, and *honesty*—so it's not that hard to remember them."

I felt like I had just confessed to cheating on a high school exam.

"I do?" she said. "Oh my, I hadn't realized that."

From that point on, she changed the words, but I still managed to remember them.

Journal entry:

> The woman in the bed next to me seems to be in very bad shape. She can't talk, and her hands are wrapped in bandages so that she won't pull out any of her IV tubes. She lies there all day, sometimes sleeping, sometimes awake, but never seems agitated as the nurses come in and roll her over to wash her. Her husband sits by her side, most of the time asking questions of her that are never answered.
>
> "Are you in pain?"
> "Do you need something?"
> And the saddest one of all, "Do you love me?"

Calling It Quits

ABOUT THREE MONTHS into my illness, I knew there was something I had to do. I couldn't keep Jack Conway in limbo without an advertising director any longer, and I had a whole year of chemo treatments ahead of me.

I put on my wig and had Al drive me into Conway headquarters to meet with Jack. When I walked into his office, he smiled but seemed a little on edge. My new look probably unnerved him, and he may have been worried about what I was going to say.

"Hello, Marie, what a surprise to see you," he said, getting up and clearing newspapers off his leather chair. "Have a seat right here. What can I do for you?"

"I'm here to give you my official letter of resignation," I said. "I'm going to be out of commission for at least a year, and the company needs an ad director."

"I'm very sorry about this, Marie," said Jack, taking the envelope from my hand and giving me a hug. "We have been a great team, but you have only one job right now, and that is to get well."

He looked sad but also a little relieved. The business came first with Jack, and I knew he needed to fill my position with a functioning human being.

It should have broken my heart to leave a job I loved so much, but nothing mattered anymore—only how horrible I was feeling. Cancer trumped everything.

"Is there anything else I can do for you, Marie?" asked Jack as I continued to sit in the chair across from him.

"Well, actually there is," I said. "Would you allow me to write some press releases for Conway on a freelance basis?" I have no idea where those words came from. I had no intention of doing anything there that day but resigning from my job. But I guess I wasn't ready to completely make the break.

"Absolutely," he said, as he took my arm and walked me into the Conway marketing department. "Attention, everyone, your boss is coming back to work for us [people started clapping], but not in her previous position. She will write stories for the company from home."

He turned to Al Becker, our publicist, who would later be promoted to my position and ultimately to Conway VP, and said, "Al, you will give Marie her assignments, and if she feels like writing, she will write. If she doesn't feel like writing, she won't. That's how it's going to be—no pressure of any kind."

It felt good to hear the protective tone in his voice.

From that point on, Al e-mailed me press release topics, and I would write them on a notepad from my hospital bed with an IV in one arm. It was a great diversion, and it made me feel somewhat productive again for the first time since the illness.

I got a handwritten letter from Jack a few days after I resigned from my job.

Marie, I know you have loved every minute of your 15 years as our Ad Director and as much as you loved it, we have loved you more. You are a person with great talent, a wonderful sense of humor, and an ability to get along with everyone in this world. Please know that you always have a friend in me and my company.

His words were kind, and they meant a lot to me.

Beautiful People and WHOPPER JRs

ONE OF THE bright lights of my monthly hospital stays were the visits of my handsome nephew Billy, Betty's oldest son, and his striking blonde fiancée, Jes.

Billy looked like a cross between JFK Jr. and Ben Affleck, and he was always meticulously dressed in a dark gray business suit and shiny black shoes. At thirty-one, he was already vice president of a major commercial real estate firm and was as nice as he was successful.

On the day I got diagnosed with the brain tumor, Billy made me a promise. "Auntie Ree, I'll come and visit you during every one of your treatments," he said. "I don't care how many you need to have. I'll be there."

He never broke that promise in the fifteen months to follow, except once when he had a meeting, and Jes came alone. They always brought me my favorite fast-food—a WHOPPER JR. burger and a medium order of fries.

My appetite was voracious from the steroids I was on, so the one perk I might have appreciated from getting cancer—weight loss—never happened. Instead of losing pounds, I was getting bigger by the minute, but I devoured those WHOPPERS anyway, and they tasted like manna from heaven.

I loved the visits of Billy and Jes, but I felt guilty about their rush-hour trips into Boston after working all day. They never complained, but they yawned a lot and were obviously bored with my less-than-scintillating conversation, which was mostly confined to the symptoms of the day. Sometimes I released them early, but I never told them not to come. I was much too needy for that.

One night after they left, I tried to go to sleep early because there was nothing better to do. I put on an eye mask and stuck earplugs in to dull the noise of people and machines. Within minutes, a new patient was wheeled into my room on a stretcher. Once she got settled and the nurses had left, the trouble began.

The poor woman kept trying to get up, not realizing that she was being restrained. People were telling her that she couldn't leave the bed without a nurse, but as soon as they left, she'd make another stab at it, setting off alarms, which brought attendants running.

In the midst of this hubbub, my nurse Linda came in to draw blood from the port in my chest. When my roommate's alarm went off, Linda panicked and ran over to the other bed, leaving blood spurting out of me like a playground bubbler. I screamed, and she ran back and ebbed the flow.

After an aide cleaned me up and helped me change into a clean nightgown, I put my eye mask back on and stuck a pillow over my head. Some spa treatment this was.

Permission to be Mad

ALLI WAS VISITING me in the hospital one night, miles from her home and her newborn son, when I saw a tense expression sweep across her face and her shoulders stiffen. I knew she was worried about me, but it was more than that.

"Are you thinking about how much you'd rather be with Benjamin right now?"

"No, Mom, I wasn't thinking that," she said with a sigh.

"Alli, I want to tell you something," I said. "If you're feeling resentful of me, you have every right to."

"Why would I resent you?" she asked.

"Because I have added a huge sorrow to your life at a time when you should be enjoying your brand-new baby. I know how you feel because I felt exactly the same way twenty-six years ago when your brother was born."

"What do you mean, Mom?" she said, leaning back against a pillow.

It was almost uncanny how much the circumstances around Jay's birth in 1982 had mirrored what was happening to me and my daughter in 2008. My son was only a couple of days old when I went over to my mother's house in Weymouth to show her the baby. I knew something was wrong the minute she answered the door. She cooed over "the young Brad Pitt" for a few minutes and then looked up at me with fear in her eyes.

"Ree, I've got troubles," she said.

"What do you mean, Ma? What's wrong?"

"I found a lump on my breast."

From that day on, my sister and I accompanied our mother through an unending nightmare of tests, biopsies, and surgeries that ended with her courageous death from breast cancer two years later.

On the day before she died, my mom had been in a semicoma at my house, where I had been caring for her with the help of hospice nurses for six weeks. They had told us that she could hear us even though she was in a coma, so Betty and I were talking to her constantly.

"Mom, we love you. Do you need anything? Are you thirsty? Just squeeze my hand."

But she never spoke a word or moved a muscle all that day.

That night I was sleeping on the couch next to my mother's bed when I heard her thrashing and calling my name. I ran to her side. "What is it, Mom? What do you need?" I said, getting close to her face.

"Let me go," she said.

"What do you mean, Ma?" I asked, scared and yet so grateful to hear her voice. "Where do you want to go?"

"To heaven."

"But I'll miss you so much," I said, bursting into tears and climbing into the bed beside her.

"Don't cry," she said. "I'll miss you too. I love you."

Those were the last words my mother ever spoke, and if I hadn't chosen to sleep on the couch next to her that night, I never would have heard them.

"Mom, do you want me to get a priest?" I asked.

She nodded her head. I was a little surprised because she was a self-described agnostic, but if she wanted the last rites, she was going to get them.

At this point in my life, religion meant nothing to me. I hadn't gone to church in years, and I was very angry with God, if there was one, for taking my mother away from me. She was only sixty-eight. Why couldn't she have lived to be eighty like her mother had or ninety-two like her grandmother?

I got out the phone book and called the local church. After six or seven rings, an old and shaky voice answered the phone.

"St. James Parish, this is Father John."

"I need you to come to my house right away to give my mother the last rites," I said.

"It's the middle of the night, madam," he said. "I will visit her in the morning and administer the sacrament of the sick."

"No, that may be too late. You have to come now. Please! I'll pay you."

The doorbell rang twenty minutes later, and in the silence of my darkened house, past rooms where my husband and babies were blissfully sleeping, I led two black-robed priests to my mother's bed. She was no longer conscious, but they started praying over her.

"Don't worry that she can't hear me," said the older one with a sly smile. "That doesn't matter. God hears me."

When the priests left, I lay back down on the couch and heard my mom's breathing start to become more shallow and spaced apart. I was suddenly filled with absolute determination that this kind and wonderful woman was not going to take her last breath in a town where nobody knew her name. My mother had adored her hometown of Arlington, where she had lived in her family home for sixty years, but she had been forced to sell the house for financial reasons after my father died in 1980.

My sister and I had convinced her to buy a little place on the South Shore closer to us, but she never adjusted and often made the long trip back to Arlington by bus and train just to see old friends and familiar faces. Her breast cancer was discovered only two months after the move.

I called Betty at 6:00 a.m. "We have to get Mom back to Arlington," I told her. "She would want that town's name on her death certificate. Will you back me up on this?"

"Yes," she said. "I'm coming right over."

I woke Al, who had slept through the entire evening's events, including the priests' arrival and departure, and told him I was taking my mother to the hospital. I called 911, and the EMTs rushed into my house with their stretcher and navy blue satchels. One of them listened to mom's heart with a stethoscope and said, "This woman barely has a pulse. We need to take her to the nearest hospital."

"No, please, she needs to be transported to the Symmes Hospital in Arlington," I said. "It's very important to her. I will take full responsibility for this."

The EMT looked from my mother to me and back again. "Well, you'll have to sign this release form saying that you have requested us to take her out of district."

"I'll sign it," I said grabbing the pen from his hand.

"But I must inform you if your mother's heart stops en route, we will have to divert to the nearest medical facility. Do you agree to that?"

"Yes, I agree."

The forty-five-minute ride to Arlington in the back of the ambulance was hellish as waves of nausea caused me to hold a pink basin to my mouth the entire time. Betty rode in front with the driver, and a female EMT kneeled next to my mother's stretcher during the bumpy journey, talking to her all the way.

"Do you believe that, Elizabeth?" she said. "Your daughter is carsick again."

My mother's courageous heart kept beating until she was settled in a bed in Arlington, where she peacefully took her last breath as my sister and I held her hands.

"I loved my mom very much, and I still miss her," I said to Alli, who was sitting on the end of my hospital bed listening to this tale of her grandmother's passing. "But I'm going to be honest with you. When I brought my newborn baby to meet her that first day, and she said, 'I've got troubles,' a part of me resented her for taking away the joy. And now by some hellish twist of fate, I've done the same thing to you. So if you resent me for it, don't you dare feel one bit guilty about it."

Alli looked down at her lap. "I don't know what you're talking about, Mom," she said. "I don't feel that way."

But her shoulders loosened, and her face relaxed. She had permission.

Advice from a Pro

LONG BEFORE I began my cancer journey, one of my coworkers, Susan Haigh, was in the midst of her own twenty-two-year struggle with stage IV breast cancer. She held a full-time job at Conway throughout her illness and never once complained about a symptom.

One day, I found her kneeling on the floor of her office doing paperwork. "Are you okay, Sue?" I asked.

"Sure, I'm fine. Just had some radiation, and it's a little painful to sit. What can I do for you, Marie?"

What she ultimately did for me was to give me the courage to make it through the shock and terror of my own cancer diagnosis. When I was sick, I would see her name come up on my cell phone every morning during the early weeks of my hospitalization.

"Just checking in on you, lady," she would say with an upbeat voice. "How much did you eat today? Remember, you have to eat. I'm going to bring over some of those dark chocolate butter creams you like so much."

After it became apparent from my girth that I was eating plenty, she changed her helpful hints to "You have to get up and move now. No matter how much you don't feel like it, just get out of bed and walk back and forth in your room. And by the way, did I tell you that you're going to be fine?"

One day, Sue offered me some sage advice while I was recounting my daily aches, pains, and fears to her on the phone.

"Marie, I know you're feeling horrible, and I want you to talk with me about it. But the next time you have visitors, ask them about what's going on in their lives. You have to try and get out of yourself a little, or this thing will swallow you up."

That night, my nephew Tommy came to visit me at the hospital. He was Betty's youngest son, and I adored him. At twenty-six, he had dark wavy hair, which he was wearing long, and a close-cropped beard, and he looked a little Christ-like as he walked into my hospital room holding an iced coffee.

"How are you feeling, Auntie Ree? Any more news from Dr. Norden?"

"Not really, Tommy, but let's talk about you tonight," I said.

Tom had graduated from Wheaton College and was now working as an accountant, but I knew he wasn't happy at his job. He was a movie addict like me and always wanted to do something in the film industry.

"So what are your goals in life, Tom? Tell me about them."

"Seriously?" he asked, with a broad smile. "Well, if you're really interested, I have a list of them. I want to study abroad for a master's degree in marketing. I really hate finance. I want to travel the world, find a job that not only makes me happy but gives me enough money to buy a house on the ocean and one in the city, and eventually find a soul mate. I can tell you more…"

Sue's advice was spot on. Hearing my nephew discuss his plans for the future was a lot more uplifting than telling him about my buzzing arm. And even to this day, Tommy will sometimes say, "Remember that night in the hospital when we talked about my goals, Auntie Ree? That was so great."

From then on, I tried to focus more on others and less on my continuing saga of distress. Sometimes I succeeded, and sometimes not.

Lesson learned: Try to take an interest in other people even if all you really want to do is wallow.

A Dope Slap

ONE MORNING, I was walking back from an MRI over the indoor "bridge" that separated Brigham and Women's Hospital from the Dana-Farber when I passed by the window of the Jimmy Fund Clinic. I could see a little girl playing at a table with some Barbie dolls. She was wearing a frilly party dress and had a pink bow taped to her bald head.

I stopped to look at her, and like a slap in the face, I realized how shamefully I had been acting. Here I was, a grandmother who had already lived a full and wonderful life, and this baby hadn't even begun. Yes, there were worse things than Marie Fricker getting brain cancer, and I was looking at one of them. At that moment in time, I knew that this child's survival meant so much more than mine, and I prayed for it, right there in the hallway. "Please, God, let this little girl live. Please, Blessed Mother. Please, Jesus."

Can I say that this wake-up call ended my "woe is me" behavior about my own illness? It certainly should have, but as the months passed and the image of that sweet child faded in my memory, I allowed self-pity to rear its pathetic head again. But from that day forward, I never asked God, my doctors, or anyone else, "Why me?"

Journal entry:

I had a good showing of visitors today, which always makes me feel better. An aide in a hunter-green uniform is mopping up and emptying wastebaskets in my room. She smiles, but I feel no need to talk with her. This is a big change from the early days of my illness. For some reason, when I first got sick, I had an unnatural curiosity about people's lives and was asking everyone for their life stories. But that seems to have passed. Now I'm only interested in knowing how they can help me. Am I regressing to the ego stage of child development? I hope it's the drugs.

Almost Human

THE ONE SYMPTOM of my illness that perplexed Dr. Norden from the beginning was my persistent "echo chamber" hearing. He said that issue was "atypical" for my disease, and he referred me to an ear, nose, and throat specialist for an exam. Alli and Jay went with me as we drove to Dr. Lin's office for the appointment.

I was feeling a little stronger that morning, and I decided to wear "normal" clothes instead of my sick person sweat suits. I chose a purple turtleneck, a black blazer, and regular jeans. Oh my god, what a feeling to look more like me again.

I was put through a variety of hearing tests much more comprehensive than that night at the Massachusetts Eye and Ear clinic and met young Dr. Lin in his office at the end of the exam.

"You have only mild hearing loss in either ear," he said. "I believe the echo you hear is caused by your lymphoma sending the wrong sensory signals from your brain. But don't worry too much. Even if your hearing remains this way, after about a year, your brain adjusts to it, and you will think your ears are normal again."

That sounded crazy then, but I can now attest that he was right. He was very interested in my case and suddenly pulled the MRI scans of my tumors onto a computer screen in his office. It was the first time I had ever seen them, and I didn't want to.

"There is the larger white spot in the thalamus and a smaller one in your right frontal lobe," he said, pointing to the image.

"Yes, but I don't really want to look at them anymore," I said.

"Okay, no problem. They're gone," he said as his screen went black. "Now please make an appointment with my secretary to come back and see me again next year."

"I don't know if I'll be alive in a year," I said, quite honestly.

"Oh no, you're not getting away with that," he said. "I want you to promise to come back and see me in a year, and you can't break a promise." He was a nice guy.

After we left his office, the kids and I went to Burtons, one of our favorite restaurants, for supper. I ordered a wedge salad with tenderloin tips, and Alli and I split a magnificent chocolate torte. Wow! This was almost like having a real life again. It must have been the clothes.

Journal entry:

Today I went to the movies for the first time since the diagnosis. Betty and I saw *Doubt*, starring Meryl Streep and Philip Seymour Hoffman. It was a sad story, and we didn't like it, but I was so grateful to be doing one of my favorite things again—sitting in a darkened theater shoulder to shoulder with a room full of strangers watching a movie.

Another Day, Another Scan

FOR WHAT SEEMED like the hundredth time, I walked into the MRI suite at the Dana-Farber for another brain scan. A technician placed a plastic mask over my face, arranged two pillows on either side of me, gave me my panic ball, and slid me into the machine like a pizza into a wood-fired oven.

I wasn't as scared as I used to be during this process. In fact, I was almost beginning to welcome the solitude of these temporary escapes from reality. No one was asking me questions, poking me with needles, or making me walk anywhere on wobbly legs. Even the clanging didn't seem as loud anymore.

It had been a couple of months since the diagnosis, and I had to admit something to myself. Being so completely disabled that people expect nothing of you can be oddly releasing. I had always been the go-to person for my family's emotional and physical problems as well as my bosses' deadlines. I had never minded those roles—in fact, I thrived on them. But now, in the dark abyss of this MRI cocoon, I was unreachable and unaccountable for anything except remaining completely still.

There is a tiny mirror inside the MRI tube that offers a glimpse of the technician in the other room during the scan, but I never look at it. My eyes are always tightly shut so that my imagination can take me anywhere I want. Sometimes I go back to the morning of October 9 when I was sitting in my car at the Scituate Lighthouse on the day before Ben was born. The sun was making the ocean sparkle like diamonds while the lighthouse loomed over it like a silent protector. Something wonderful was about to happen in my life, and I couldn't wait to watch it unfold. I know now that God had other plans for me, but thinking back on the anticipation of that morning always makes me happy.

On the Home Front

In the early months, when I wasn't at the hospital getting treatments, I was dragging my butt around my house feeling, and almost wishing, that each day of this abject misery would be my last. It occurred to me one morning how little I had valued one of the most wonderful daily routines of my life—going through the drive-through lane at Dunkin' Donuts and ordering a small coffee with milk and no sugar. If I ever got better, I would never take that mindless task for granted again.

I couldn't drive my car now, even if my doctor had allowed it. My reflexes were too slow, and my head too fuzzy. I was relegated to the passenger seat and was happy to be hauled around by anyone who wanted my dubious company—usually my sister, who had a dull sidekick for all her daily errands. For the first time, I realized how horrible it must have been for my sister-in-law Sue, who couldn't get a driver's license because of her epilepsy, to live her whole life dependent on others for transportation. She used to tell me about how hard it was, but I never sympathized enough. I would from now on.

Since the visit with Dr. Lin, I had tried to accept my muffled, echo hearing, but it was unbearable if I went to a restaurant or other loud places. I could hear other people's conversations overlapping one another like a discordant cacophony of musical instruments tuning up for a concert.

"I really can't take this Al. It's driving me crazy," I said on our first trip as a family to our local sports café. I have to get out of here now."

"Okay, Ree, calm down. We'll get our dinners to go. It's okay."

At home, I had to struggle with the opposite problem. I couldn't hear any dialogue on a television show unless I had the volume sky high, which blasted everyone else out of the room. As usual, it was Jay who came up with the solution.

"Check these babies out, Ma," he said, holding out a box that said "TV Ears" on the outside. "I saw these on a commercial, and they look like just what you need. They were on sale at Walmart."

He handed me a miraculous headphone device that allowed me to turn the TV volume up as loud as I wanted while it remained at a normal level for everyone else. I loved this thing and wore it constantly. "Hey, Al, if anything goes wrong and I don't make it through this," I said, "put the TV Ears on me in the casket. It might get a laugh."

Lesson learned: For every symptom, search for a remedy. You might even find it at Walmart.

The Door Is Open

SINCE MY CANCER battle had begun, friends and strangers came in and out of my house at will—the visiting nurse, the physical therapist, neighbors, cable men, social workers. I couldn't get up and down to let them in, so I just left the door unlocked. The message to anyone who could help me was, "Come on in. The door is open."

One of the less welcome early visitors to my house was Edith, a tall, somber-faced physical therapist who had been assigned to my case. Just getting up from the couch and making it to the bathroom was physical therapy enough for me, but this woman insisted that I do a series of exercises at her command.

"Lie on your bed and bend your feet up and down at the ankles," she would say like a drill sergeant. "Lift one leg, tighten your thigh and buttock muscles, bend both knees, and put your feet on the bed. Now lift your hips."

"This is really hard," I whined.

"Well, nothing worthwhile is ever easy, is it, Mrs. Fricker?"

Edith held my elbow as we walked around my house in circles, and she made me march in place at the kitchen sink. We always ended our little "workouts" with a stroll around my small cul-de-sac while I pushed the walker ahead of me. Dogs in the neighborhood who have known me for years barked at us as I made my slow and painful journey up and down the street.

My tortured expression caused my neighbor Ted to yell out from his window one morning, "Hey Marie, are you training for the marathon again? Do you know this woman? Should we call the police?" I laughed but secretly wished that Edith would disappear into an open sewer grate.

I dreaded her visits so much that I sometimes thought of locking the door and pretending I wasn't home, but I always let her in, silently cursing her arrival. Eventually, she determined that I had made enough progress and released me from her torturous tutelage.

Looking back on my physical therapy stint with Edith, I realize she was only trying to help me. Maybe I should have baked her some brownies on that last day. But I did wave good-bye with a smile on my face. Maybe she thought I had enjoyed her, but it was really just relief.

Lesson learned: When therapists torture you, just grin and bear it. Eventually, they leave.

Journal entry:

I woke up at 6:45 a.m., alone in the house, and managed to make it to the bathroom without using the walker. The chest pressure I'd been feeling from the steroids was pretty intense, and I couldn't get back to sleep.

Denise [Ted's wife] called to make sure I had taken my 9:00 a.m. pills. Benjamin had his first sleepover at my house with Alli. I can't take much of an interest in him although I want to. The only way I'll hold him is if I sit on the couch with pillows propped on all sides because I'm so unsure of myself. Poor Ben. It's a good thing he's too young to realize how shortchanged he is on a grandmother.

At lunchtime, Sandi [another neighbor] came over with a huge pot of Italian wedding soup, and Chris [neighbor number 3] brought me a shepherd's pie for supper. I hate shepherd's pie, but it was nice of her to bring it. I'm becoming a burden to my entire neighborhood, but I'm too desperate to care.

The three musketeers—Betty, Mom, and me in 1960.

I'm on the left in this Easter Sunday photo
on Teel Street in Arlington, 1959.

My father, Henry Gallishaw, the smartest
and funniest man I've ever known.

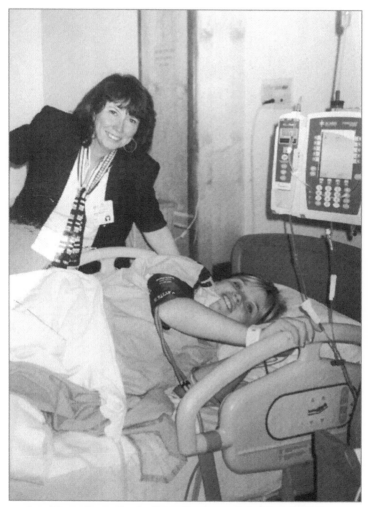

Awaiting the arrival of my first grandchild with Alli on
October 10, 2008. I had a brain tumor but didn't know it.

Before the diagnosis. I felt like I was dying, and I was.

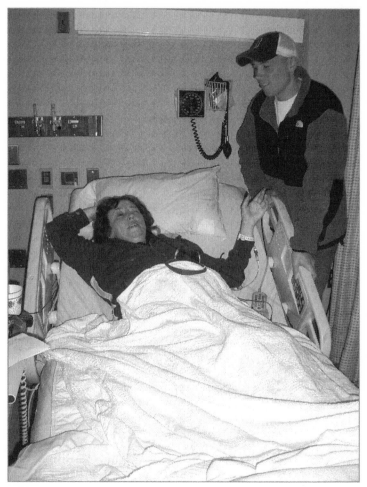

Still no answers. Poor Jay was a saint.

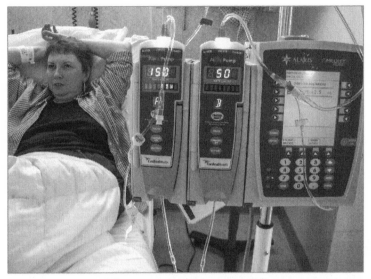

My not so brave new world.

At the hospital cafe with my chest port showing and my
IV pole behind me. Must have been appetizing for others.

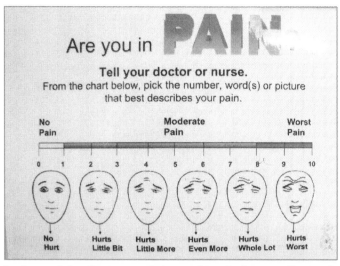

A piece of the fine artwork in my hospital room. Seriously, how annoying is the face of Mr. "Hurts Worst?"

I wrote this article for *Pug Talk* magazine about Sammy, my black pug who died of a brain tumor two months before I got mine.

Wearing my "TV Ears" with Otis and Maxine. My new
hair feels a lot like steel wool, but I'm thrilled to have it.

My sister Betty and her boys, Tom
and Billy, were always there.

My gorgeous daughter Alli and her steroid-ridden mother.

Wearing my Raquel Welch wig with the new guy in my life.

Bloating from steroids and chemo made me
unrecognizable to myself and others.

My nephew Billy and his fiancée, Jes,
my most frequent visitors.

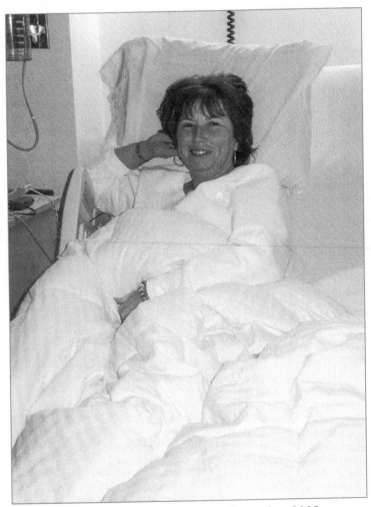

The final chemo treatment—December 2009.

Scituate Light, my safe harbor in the storm.

Back to work in 2010. Can you tell I'm scared?

The late Jack Conway, an icon in Massachusetts real estate.

The fabulous foursome—Alli, Al, me and Jay.

When the flock disperses, the faithful remain.
From left: Susan, me, Chris and Joyce (seated).

Hollywood Walk of Fame - 2011 - two years in remission.

Presenting Jay with the MVP award
at the PCNSL After-Party.

Sisters - 2011

Appearing with Dr. Norden at the
Jimmy Fund Telethon in 2010.

An Easter selfie with the family, celebrating five years in
remission! How cute is my Benji and his little brother Will?

The "before and after" poster from my after-party.

So happy with Jay on his wedding day, 2012.

Me and my hero after an "all-clear" MRI.
"See you next year!"

Benjamin James Kieffner—the prize!
(Photo by Andrea Gardner Photography)

Exit Mother Teresa

IN THE EARLY weeks of my illness, my kids started calling me Mother Teresa because I had become a soft-spoken, saintly individual who never said a bad word against another human being. It wasn't like I was ever mean to others, but I hadn't been above pointing out someone's flaws to get a laugh. I was known for being funny, and I would say almost anything when I had an audience.

My father had a similar sense of humor, and I thought he was hysterical. He had secret nicknames for people such as my godfather, Carmine, who bore an uncanny resemblance to a sumo wrestler-type villain named Oddjob in the James Bond movie *Goldfinger*. If my godparents were coming over for a visit, I'd hear him say to my mother, "Oh, for God sakes, Betty, we just saw those Oddjobs last week. They'll eat us out of house and home."

On every New Year's Eve, my parents watched the Times Square festivities on TV led by the increasingly decrepit bandleader Guy Lombardo. But at midnight, no matter what the weather was, my mom would go out onto our front porch and blow a horn or clang a pan with a metal spoon. She said you had to make noise to see the New Year in. My father would just sit in his chair and shake his head. "Your mother's a nutcase," he'd say with a smile. "Betty, you better get in here. They're about to stick Guy Lombardo back into the mothballs for another year."

My mother, who was literally the kindest person in the world, didn't appreciate her husband's deprecating sense of humor. "I don't find your father funny at all," she would say, "because he's always belittling someone else, and I don't like that."

Actually the sting of his wit hit me broadside one night as I was walking by him in the living room as he sat in his chair playing chess on a small magnetic lap board.

"Hey, daughter," he yelled out. "Please accept my apologies."

"What do you mean?"

"It appears you may have inherited the Gallishaw wall-to-wall ass. But don't worry about it. My mother and sister had it, and they made out okay."

And then he laughed demonically, showing his two huge dimples.

As a self-conscious adolescent, I didn't find that one bit funny, but if it had been said about anyone else, it probably would have cracked me up.

I guess I had inherited more from my father than his dimples and the Gallishaw wall-to-wall ass.

But when the tumors struck and I was barely able to function, I felt an overwhelming urge to become a better person. And for a while, I did. Nothing but compliments and gratitude came from my lips about anyone and everyone.

"Geez, Ma, I kind of miss the old you," said Alli one day during this period of sainthood. "Your critiques of other people were always a riot."

My desire to be less judgmental was an absolutely obsessive thought in my mind during the early weeks. It was like a veil had been lifted, and I had seen the error of my ways. I don't know if it was God sending me a lesson or the brain tumor stirring up trouble, but like Ebenezer Scrooge on the morning after his ghostly admonitions, I was determined to change.

And then came the cable man. He was a red-faced, sweating guy with a beer gut and gin blossoms (my father's term for broken blood vessels on the face) who was putting a new phone jack in the living room because I had become paranoid about not having a landline available at every moment of the day. I was sitting in my cushioned glider wrapped in a blue electric blanket while Jay told him where we wanted the jack to go.

This guy was whipping my front door open and closed repeatedly going to and from his truck for unknown reasons on the coldest day of the year. After his last grand entrance, he kneeled on the floor, closed the lid of his toolbox, and looked up at my son.

"I'm gonna have to come back on Monday," he said. "I don't have the right part with me. Sorry about that."

"Are you kidding?" said Jay. "Are we gonna have to pay for this service call?"

"Well, I spent two hours here, didn't I? Do you work for nothing, buddy?" And with that he walked out of the house, stepping on Otis's back paw with his heavy work boot and evoking a high-pitched yelp that he never acknowledged.

"Do you believe that guy?" said Jay, picking up our pug and patting him.

"He was a moron," I said as naturally as spitting out a cherry pit. "And we aren't paying him one cent for today."

"Oh my god," said Jay, throwing his head back and laughing. "She's back! Bye, bye, Mother Teresa."

Lesson learned: You think you're going to become a better person when catastrophe strikes, and you do, for a while, but gradually the old you worms its way back. Sainthood is short-lived, at least it was for me.

Bless Me, Father, Please

LIVING LESS THAN thirty miles from Boston, I had the advantage of battling my brain tumor with the help of a world-class medical institution. Dana-Farber/Brigham and Women's Cancer Center is ranked in the top five in the country among hospitals of its kind. I had faith in the treatment I was getting there, but it was faith of a different sort that brought me down the street from the Longwood Medical area to another Boston landmark on a wintry afternoon.

On the way home from an early chemo treatment, Betty and I stopped in at the renowned Basilica of Our Lady of Perpetual Help, better known as the Mission Church, on Tremont Street in Roxbury. Gaining fame through the years for its miraculous healings, this was the church where Senator Ted Kennedy came to pray for his daughter Kara when she was diagnosed with lung cancer and from which he would be buried after succumbing to a brain tumor in 2009.

My sister and I walked into the magnificent gothic structure with its towering arches and famous shrine to the Blessed Mother, which is flanked on each side by giant "vases" filled with discarded crutches, canes, and braces. Father Edward McDonough, who had died just nine months earlier, had been known as the Healing Priest, and he was said to have cured many people of their illnesses through the intercession of Mary.

There were about thirty people scattered about in the church's pews, but no Mass or service was going on, and our footsteps echoed in the voluminous surrounds of the basilica. A faint smell of incense was in the air.

"Couldn't Father McDonough have hung on for a few more months to help me out?" I whispered. I laughed to downplay the irreverence, but I actually meant it.

"Let's see if they have a gift shop here," said Betty after we said some prayers, lit a candle, and left the main church. My sister would be able to sniff out a gift shop in the bowels of hell, and this was no exception. We walked into the Mission Church's store, and she bought some wooden rosary beads. She didn't go to Mass anymore, but she was a parochial school girl and still believed.

"Can we get these beads blessed?" said Betty to the store clerk, a gray-haired woman in a flowered smock. "My sister has brain cancer, and she needs them."

I cringed when the words *brain cancer* came out of her mouth. It sounded like such a death sentence. The clerk, who had been gazing at us with an air of indifference suddenly perked up and said, "You girls are in luck. Here comes Father. Maybe he will have time to give you a blessing."

The priest, who was elderly and slightly hunched, attempted to pass by us on his way out a door, but Betty stood in his path and would have tackled him if he took another step. I felt like Tiny Tim in a Christmas Carol as she said, "Please Father, can you help my sister?" He asked what was wrong with me, and my favorite phrase once again escaped her lips: "She has brain cancer."

His expression never changed, but he laid his hands on my head and said a long prayer. I don't remember any of the words, but the litany ended with "God bless you, sister." I didn't feel any differently when he was done, not even the sensation of heat I got when a sweet chaplain named Heather performed Reiki on me one night in the hospital or the calmness that swept over me when Chris Berlin, the head chaplain at the Brigham, swept a wooden mallet across the rim of a "Tibetan singing bowl" while guiding me in a bedside meditation.

The truth was that I felt nothing at all from this healing priest's hands or the prayer he uttered. I just hoped that Our Lady of Perpetual Help would stay true to her name and send me some much-needed assistance from above. Looking back on it now, I know that she did.

Lesson learned: Pray hard and often. Seek help on earth and in heaven.

Who's That in the Mirror?

ANOTHER DEPRESSING FEATURE of having cancer was that not only did I no longer feel like myself, I no longer looked like myself either—not even close.

If I caught a glimpse of my reflection in a store window or mirror, I would see a puffy, bloated face where there once had been cheekbones and discernible features. My hair was scant and patchy, with the consistency of steel wool. My chins numbered two and a half, and I was getting bigger by the day.

"I thought people with cancer were supposed to be emaciated," I said to Dr. Norden one day.

"Well, apparently not always," he said with a wink.

During one of my hospital stays, some friends from my office brought me a gift of a lap desk that was wrapped in shiny silver paper with a purple bow. They were graphic designers, and one of them had cleverly cloned a photo of the "precancer me" over the face of the model on the cover of the box.

Seeing myself in that picture with my thick brown hair and smiling face was depressing. The person in that photo had been happy, healthy, and leading a normal life.

"Oh, you guys shouldn't have done this," I said, totally meaning it. "But it was so nice of you."

Back at home a short time later, I walked into the Jack Conway real estate office in my hometown and greeted the agent who was manning the front desk. I had known Ed for years, and I expected a warm greeting from him. What I got was, "Can I help you, ma'am?"

"Are you serious?" I asked.

"Is there something I can do for you?"

"Oh my god, Ed, you really don't know me?"

At that point, he must have recognized my voice. "Marie?" he said, staring intently at my face. "You just look so different. What am I saying? Get over here." And he jumped up from his desk and gave me a hug. "I'm so sorry I didn't recognize you. You look great."

"Yeah, sure, Ed. Thanks."

Lesson learned: Avoid mirrors and old acquaintances until you look more like you.

Some Grandmother

Young Benjamin Kieffner saw me in my normal, functioning–human being state just once—on the day he was born. I had looked into his incredibly blue eyes that night and promised him a lifetime of devotion. Less than a week later, I couldn't have handed him a rattle.

I never dreamed that my grandson would first come to know me as an invalid. In the early days of the illness, I showed no interest in the baby when my daughter would bring him to my house for visits. If Alli placed him in my arms, as she insisted on doing, I was petrified the whole time that I might drop or injure him. My fears came true one day when I was wearing reading glasses on a chain around my neck (a new old lady habit I had acquired since the tumor) and the frame poked him in the eye and made him cry.

"Take him back," I said bursting into tears. "Don't you see I can't do this, Alli? I can't be a grandmother. I want to, but I can't."

Before Ben's birth, I had made great plans for the wonderful kind of grandparent I would be to this precious little boy. I knew one thing for sure—he would never call me Nana because I had disliked (okay, maybe even detested) my own Nana, who had lived with us until I was fourteen years old. My maternal grandmother, May Lee, lived with our family until she died of a stroke in 1967. She was a strong, hardworking woman, but a total menace to the happiness and tranquility of our household.

She and her husband, Tom, the grandfather I never met, had inadvertently produced my mother in 1916 and dropped her off on Tom's mother's doorstep (well, not actually on the doorstep—they did carry her inside) when she was three months old so they could continue their wild life in New York City. From what my mom said, her father was warm and loving to her when he and Nana would make their sporadic visits to her house throughout the years, and she adored him. Nana, who had a drug and alcohol addiction that she later kicked, was mean and vindictive and, for some unknown reason, loved to torment her only child, who never deserved it.

May had been the oldest daughter of five children in a very poor Irish household. Her mother died when she was eleven and her alcoholic father when she was nineteen. She ran away as a teenager and supposedly had three husbands, all of whom had left her a widow. (I wondered if death was their only means of escape.) I honestly think that she was a very unhappy, unloved woman, and she resented the fact that her daughter was not.

Nana liked to plan her verbal attacks for moments when my mom was particularly enjoying life, like on holidays and other occasions when laughter would emanate from the downstairs up to the second floor where she was living. The signal of an onslaught about to occur would be the sound of heavy footsteps plodding down the stairs.

"Oh no, here she comes," my mother would say nervously. "We're in for it now."

Nana would stride into the room from the hallway with her hands on her hips like a Gestapo guard with her tightly permed white hair, stiffly starched house dress, and black tie shoes. She had a square, stocky build but wasn't plump and big-breasted like my mother.

"What are you people doing, playing your little, piddling games again?" she would say, referring to my parents' nightly Scrabble tournaments at the kitchen table. "I see the old ladies at the nursing home playing that silly game all the time." (Nana worked as a chambermaid at The Morville House, a home for rich elderly women in Boston, until she was seventy-five years old. On two occasions, she supported our family when my father was out of work recuperating from heart surgery, but she always made sure that the world knew about her sacrifice.)

After ridiculing the game they were playing, the attack would become much more personal. "I saw Mrs. Breslin [a neighbor] on my way home from work yesterday," she told my mother one night. "She was asking me why she hadn't seen your husband at the bus stop lately. I told her that he was sick again and I was carrying the whole household. Well, what do you expect, I said. My daughter married a cripple."

My father pounded the table, sending the Scrabble pieces soaring. "Get the hell back upstairs, you mean son of a bitch," he said, pointing at Nana with the veins popping out of his neck.

She just muttered, "Well it's true," and shuffled down the hallway. Her job was done. There was no more laughter.

So for these and many other reasons, my grandson would not be calling me Nana.

Journal entry:

The MRI waiting room today has ten people in it, some patients, some companions—sons, daughters, spouses. A translucent wall with yellow leaves separates the waiting area from the check-in desk.

I write down two questions I must remember to ask Dr. Norden the next time I see him:

1. I feel down a lot, and Jay thinks I should be on an antidepressant. Should I?
2. Do you think I'm going to live?

I know he won't answer question 2, but I ask it anyway, every time I see him.

With a Little Help from My Friends

Two months into the illness, when the flock of well-wishers had dispersed, a few die-hards remained for the long haul. My good friends Joyce and Susan, who worked with me when I was a PR writer for the Massachusetts Department of Education sixteen years before, visited every weekend.

Joyce, the tech genius, put all my medical information—appointments, treatments, scans, medications, and daily doses—into her laptop and provided me with weekly printouts.

"I know you'll never be able to keep track of all of this yourself," she said, trying to be gruff. "You and Susan are both the same—totally disorganized."

Susan brought snacks, gave hugs, took the dog out, and offered TLC.

"When you don't feel well, don't try to be brave for us," she would say. "We aren't here to be entertained. We're here to help. If you want to sleep, we'll leave. You can't hurt our feelings."

My friend Brenda, an older woman who used to be my children's babysitter, came to the house daily for seven long months. Hearing her walk in at 7:30 a.m. while I was up in my bedroom alone made me feel safe. I'd yell down, "Brenda, is that you?"

"No, it's the boogeyman. Time to rise and shine."

She would push Otis out to the deck, feed him, and change his water. Then she'd vacuum the rugs, clean the kitchen, and put a bowl of cereal and blueberries on the table. I offered to pay her for what she did, but she just said, "That's nonsense. I do this because I love you."

Even some people I had known long ago reemerged to help me in my time of need. Sally, a woman I hadn't seen in thirty years, called every day to check on how I was doing and visited me in the hospital twice. John, a retired colleague from the Department of Education, offered to host a fund-raiser for me to help with medical bills. I wouldn't have accepted that, nor did I need it, because I had a wonderful insurance plan through Al's Teamster's Union, but it was nice of him to ask.

Richard, a college classmate I had recently reconnected with through Facebook, e-mailed me unbelievable words of encouragement almost every day. My childhood best friend Donna called regularly, Al's sister Christine cleaned my house and took over my online banking, and cards poured in from everywhere.

The love and support I was getting from so many people during this illness reminded me of a much earlier time in my life when friends and family saw me through another crisis.

It was the summer of 1964, and I had just turned eleven.

I lived on Teel Street in Arlington, a suburb about six miles north of Boston. Our neighborhood led from the town's main thoroughfare, Mass Avenue, to St. Paul's Cemetery at the end. Abutting the graveyard was Waldo Park, where we rode our bikes, skated, played hide and seek, and spent every waking hour of our childhood summers.

From early July until the end of August, the playground ran a recreational program led by two "teachers" who were actually college students. They taught us how to make potholders and molds and weave bracelets out of gimp. They held costume parades, talent shows, and weenie roasts. But the biggest draw of the summer program was the Nok Hockey game that was the envy of every kid in town. It was just a three-by-four-foot wooden board with two holes cut out for goals, two eight-inch hockey sticks, and a puck, but we loved it. We vied for the title of Nok Hockey champion every summer.

There was a sign-up sheet on the Waldo Park fence that allowed people to take the game home for the weekend, and on one Saturday afternoon in July, it was all mine. Whoever had custody of the Nok Hockey board was a VIP among their peers, and my yard was packed with neighborhood kids waiting for a turn. Noticing my gang of friends so engrossed in the game, I decided to entertain the crowd by climbing to the top of one of our big elm trees.

"Look at me, look at me. I'm a jungle girl from the age of three." Yes, I actually said that.

I put one foot on a short branch that was jutting out from the tree in the shape of a slingshot. When I added my other foot to the limb, I felt it snap, and my body plummeted to the ground, whizzing through leaves and sticks and landing on the grass with a thud. At first, I tried to get up because I didn't want to cry in front of the kids, but when I heard them scream, I looked down and screamed along with them. My left thigh had turned into a sprawling, misshapen mass with something hard protruding beneath the skin.

I had broken my femur (the largest bone in the body) and had to spend a month in traction in the pediatric ward of Symmes Hospital and then another month in a body cast that left me completely immobile. The cast wrapped around the middle of my chest and went all the way down one leg to the ankle and down the other to the knee.

My mom gave up her part-time job as a clerk at Maida's Drugstore to take care of me. "Are you ready to take me on at Crazy Eights?" she'd say with a smile, dealing the cards out on a plastic cutting board she would place on top of my chest. "Or would you rather play Yahtzee today?"

I can still remember the feel of her smooth warm hand in mine and the cold face cloths she would lay on my forehead on hot summer nights.

I often wondered if my mother would have been the same loving and selfless person that she was if she had been raised by her carousing, bar-hopping parents instead of by her doting grandmother, Elizabeth. A black-haired, blue-eyed beauty from Georgia, Elizabeth (Dasher) Lee, had relocated to Boston as a young widow with her teenaged son Tom in 1901. She and her husband, Dorsey, had had a second child, Joseph, who was run over and killed by a horse-drawn cart when he was only four years old. Maybe she viewed getting an infant granddaughter to raise twenty-five years later as God's way of making up to her for the tragic loss of her boy.

Elizabeth worked as a housekeeper for a wealthy family, saved every penny, and at age 60, was able to buy the house on Teel Street where she raised my mother, and where my sister and I would later grow up.

While I was recuperating from my broken leg in the stifling August of 1964, my parents would haul me from my bed to a foldable stretcher and wheel me out to the front porch to get some fresh air and "hold court" with the kids on the street. There was not a single day of that long hot month that at least one childhood friend wasn't sitting by my side.

They kept me company and gave me the patience to make it to the long-awaited moment when the whirring of an orthopedist's buzz saw spewing white plaster freed me from the prison of my cast and I could walk again.

And now, forty-four years later, my friends and family were once again supporting me through the toughest battle of my life.

Lesson learned: Author Kris Carr referred to her circle of supporters as a "posse" in her book The Crazy Sexy Cancer Survivor, *but whatever you call it, having a team on your side is invaluable.*

Journal entry:

I think my grandson likes me. Ben is almost four months old, and I am three months into treatment. I'm still extremely weak and can't do much with him, but something has changed. When he comes to my house with his mother now, he looks directly into my eyes with his huge blue ones and smiles. Somehow, he knows that this zombie of a woman bundled in a green glider with a million blankets on her belongs to him and that she loves him. I can't walk around with him like his other grandmother can. I can't get down on the floor and play with him, but somehow he senses that he's mine and that I am his.

Burnt Again

WHILE RECUPERATING AT home after my monthly treatments, I burned myself twice on hot pot handles because I couldn't feel the heat with my numb left hand, so I learned to steer clear of cooking. Brenda would boil six eggs for me on Sunday nights and put them in the refrigerator so that I could have them during the week.

I loved eggs but was sick of eating them cold, so one day I decided to peel one of them and zap it in the microwave. When the timer went off, I used a potholder and carefully took the egg out of the oven. I felt it with my good hand, and it was barely warm, so I popped it into my mouth and bit into it. With the sound of a balloon popping, the egg exploded inside my mouth scorching my lower lip before I could spit it out in a million pieces.

After holding an ice pack against the burn for hours, I wound up with a huge white blister.

"Oh my god, Al," I yelled from the bathroom, looking at my lip in the medicine chest mirror. "Come and see this thing. It's never gonna heal with my pathetic immune system. Do you think it will kill me?"

"That's ridiculous," he said. "But maybe you should e-mail Dr. Norden and tell him about it."

He was just as paranoid as I was. Jay was right. My neuroses were contagious.

Journal entry:

I got a phone call from Alli tonight sounding scared. She said she was working out on her elliptical machine and suddenly had shortness of breath and a rapid heartbeat. She almost made Jeremy call 911, but then it passed. I told her it was probably just anxiety. She is a new mother, and her own mother has brain cancer— that oughta do it. Unfortunately, Alli has inherited my hypochondria, which was transferred to me as a child through my sister Betty, who established the trend. Of course, with my current diagnosis, my gravestone will probably read, "I told you so."

Like Mother, Like Daughter

MY FIRSTBORN CHILD, Allison Elizabeth Fricker, entered the world in November of 1979 at a time when I desperately needed her. Al and I had been married for three years, and during that entire time, he had worked night shifts and weekends, which meant I lived alone in a town forty miles from a familiar face. I returned home from my job in Boston every night, ate supper alone, and went to bed. My sister lived in New Hampshire, my parents didn't drive, and my friends actually had on-site husbands.

Sometimes, when I didn't want to go home to an empty house, I would drive to Arlington and sit out in my parents' screen porch with them on summer nights.

"Hey, look," my father would say as he saw me walking up the driveway to the yard. "It's the little wanderer again. Maybe we should adopt her."

I found out I was pregnant with Alli while I was working in the PR department at the Massachusetts Department of Education. I told my colleague Chris that I was going to call my doctor's office to get the results of my blood test, and I swore her to secrecy.

"I'll tell you if I am. But you can't tell a soul, not anyone. Promise?"

She agreed, and I made the call.

A nurse answered and put me on hold while she looked up my results. "Your test was positive, Mrs. Fricker. You are pregnant."

I dropped the phone on the desk and yelled out to everyone in the office, "I'm having a baby!"

Chris just looked at me and laughed. "Don't worry, Marie, I won't tell a soul."

When Alli was born, she instantly became my best friend and the love of my life, but Al didn't seem to mind taking a backseat to this new arrival. He worshiped her too, and he was probably relieved that I now had someone other than him to rely upon for companionship. The son of two unemotional parents, he was independent and a bit of an island while I was the clinging product of a mother who had been a lonely only child and idolized her two daughters above all else.

"I have the two smartest, most beautiful girls in the world," she would say to anyone who would listen. "And they're as nice as they are pretty."

I could never quite understand why the public at large didn't seem quite as impressed with my beauty and brilliance as my mom appeared to be, but it was nice to have a number 1 fan at home.

It was only natural then that as a mother myself, I should dote on my firstborn child and later her golden-haired brother. My kids were never more than an arm's length from me during their childhood years, and when Alli left for Providence College, I cried for a week.

"It's time to cut the umbilical cord," my friend Joyce would say. "Your daughter is grown up now and has her own life. You have to let her go."

What was this—some rehabilitated dolphin that I was releasing to the sea? No, this was my little girl, and I wasn't ready to let her go, not yet. Unfortunately, I never was ready, and I may have made her more dependent on me than I should have.

Alli graduated from Providence College with honors, became a teacher, married the man of her dreams, and now had a baby of her own, but I knew she still needed her mother. Did I make a terrible mistake in keeping her so close?

If I died, would she make it without me?

Seeking Survivors

DURING ONE OF my hospital stays, I picked up a pamphlet about a telephone support program at the Dana-Farber. One-To-One is a volunteer-staffed service that connects current patients with survivors of their specific type of cancer. I was psyched. I would be thrilled to talk with someone who had battled my illness and was still alive.

I called the number on the pamphlet and asked to speak to a survivor of primary central nervous system lymphoma. Unfortunately, my disease is so rare that there was no One-to-One volunteer in Massachusetts who had ever had PCNSL.

"Now don't lose hope," said Joshua, the program's coordinator. "I'm going to check with our affiliate hospitals and find someone for you, even if we have to go to California."

Eddie

About a week later, Joshua called and gave me the name of a PCNSL survivor named Eddie, who had received treatment in his home state of Texas. He was a volunteer counselor through the MD Anderson Cancer Center, and I called him that night. Eddie was a sixty-year-old ex-cop who had been diagnosed with my illness eight years ago, so when he said he was just recently able to walk without a cane, I wasn't thrilled. What kind of pep talk was this going to be? But then again, he was alive, and that's all that mattered.

"When I got sick, my doctors told me I wasn't going to make it," said Eddie, speaking slowly and deliberately due to a deficit from either the tumor or the chemo. "But I proved them wrong. I knew I could beat it, and I did."

He was sweet and wanted to help me, but he definitely had some issues. He was hard of hearing and couldn't remember much, so after a while, he gave the phone to his wife, Linda, who filled me on every detail of her husband's battle with his brain tumor.

"You call me anytime you're feeling scared," said Eddie, taking the phone back from Linda at the end of our conversation. "And I'll tell you why you shouldn't be."

Carla

I appreciated finding Eddie, but I wanted to talk with more PCNSL survivors who could share their stories. Dr. Norden ferreted one out who was much closer to home. Carla had been diagnosed at another major Boston hospital eleven years ago, and despite two recurrences, she was currently in remission.

My sister and I met up with her at a Friendly's Restaurant on a drizzly afternoon. She was a tall, youthful-looking sixty-nine-year old with a thick mane of curly red hair. "The doctor told me I would go bald from the chemo," she said. "But I told him, 'No I won't,' and I never did." *(Why hadn't I tried that?)*

Carla's tumor went into remission after her second treatment, stayed that way for five years, and then relapsed, not once but twice, putting her back in high-dose chemotherapy for extended periods. She had been cancer-free this time around for about four years and considered herself cured.

"Aren't you afraid of what your next MRI will show?" I asked.

"I believe in the power of prayer, and I know God will get me through any ordeal," she said. "I wasn't scared when they told me I had a brain tumor, and I'm not scared now."

I felt comforted by this rosy-faced woman who was wolfing down her Friendly's hamburger and shake. We met up a couple of times later, and on bad nights, I would call her just to hear her voice. When she'd pick up the phone, I'd say, "Just wanted to see how you are," but what I really meant was, "Just wanted to make sure you're still alive."

Lesson learned: Find survivors of your disease. If they made it, you can too.

Journal entry:

Just got back from the hairdresser's. Daniel brought me to a special station so I wouldn't have to climb the *Gone with the Wind* staircase to the second floor. There was a little curtain around it for privacy. He gave me a haircut that made me look like a Holocaust victim but said it was the best he could do. Al and I went to Betty's house afterward for pizza. She had bought me a pair of size XXL jeans, which were huge in the legs but fit fine around my ever-expanding waist. No allergic reaction to blame this time. I've officially become the Stay Puft Marshmallow Man.

Cyber Support

Since Carla and Eddie were my only go-to survivors of PCNSL, one night I turned to the web and made an incredible find: an online support group for people with primary central nervous system lymphoma. I read about the group, its history, and mission and submitted a request to become a member. It was accepted almost immediately.

The site was started by a man named Barry Gates, who was a four-time survivor of my disease. Barry had to undergo chemotherapy, whole brain radiation, and a stem cell transplant. He is blind in one eye and permanently disabled, but he continues to host the website and help others cope.

Some nights I would just read what other survivors were saying in the group, and sometimes I would make comments. I introduced myself in my first post and gave a summary of my diagnosis and treatment.

"I am really scared right now, and anything that anyone can say to give me hope would be much appreciated," I wrote at the end of the message. "Once I'm a little more together, I will do the same for you." I made good on that promise in the years that followed and continue to do so today, both on

Barry's site and on the PCNSL Facebook page ("I Survive Brain Tumors") that spun off from it.

"Of course you're scared, Marie," said Barry in his response to my post. "We are coping with cancer in our brain, the center of our awareness, our memory, our intelligence, and our soul. That's something that very few cancer patients have to deal with. We wonder if we'll be able to think, see, walk, or talk tomorrow. It's natural to be frightened, but there is so much reason to have hope as well."

I told Barry about the gloomy survival statistics I had read online.

"Don't let the numbers scare you," he said. "The dataset they use can be as much as 20 years old. Back then, PCNSL was a death sentence, but great advances have been made in the last seven years."

"What else can you tell me?" I asked, wanting to jump through the computer and into his arms.

"In 2002 when I got diagnosed, they said my life expectancy with treatment was 19 months," he said. "Well, here I am seven years later. You're winning the battle, Marie. Keep up your hope and don't lose sight of your future."

Future? Could I really have a future?

My discovery of Barry's site brought with it a small but invaluable treasure trove of other PCNSL survivors—about twenty of them in total from New York to Singapore. They ranged in age from their midthirties to seventy-nine.

Most of these people were like myself—shell-shocked from their diagnosis, scared of dying, and desperately seeking hope. I got to know them through their posts and over time developed online relationships that both uplifted and upset me.

Lyn, Age 50, from Minnesota

Lyn was a long-distance runner and cyclist who had been diagnosed with her brain tumor at the same time that I was, so we felt an immediate kinship. She had gone into remission after getting chemotherapy and was doing well, except for some paralysis in one leg that caused her to walk with a cane. Like me, she was terrified of dying, and we often traded symptoms and posted back and forth about our progress.

Lyn was a gay woman of Japanese descent who lived with her partner Barbara in Minneapolis. They were big-time health enthusiasts, bikers, hikers, and runners, and she was still reeling from the shock of getting cancer in her brain.

"Sometimes I just can't believe it, Marie," she said one day in a private message to me. "I did everything right. No red meat, no fats, exercising all the time. How did this happen to me?"

"I don't know, Lyn, because it happened to me, and I don't do any of those things," I said.

"How long do you think it will be before we can feel that we're in the clear—two years or so?"

"The only thing I know is that the longer you get clear MRIs, the more likely you are to stay that way. That's all my doctor will tell me."

"There's just so much I still want to do," said Lyn.

"Yeah, tell me about it."

During this time, I made friends with a few other people in the group, and months went by before I noticed that Lyn's name was missing from all the recent posts. I e-mailed her repeatedly but got no response, so I decided to call her at home. Barbara answered the phone. When I told her my name, she recognized it right away.

"Marie, you have helped Lyn so much. It's so good to hear from you," she said. "But I'm afraid she can't come to the phone to talk with you right now. She's having some cognitive issues, and her speech is affected. Two months ago, she went for a routine MRI and was told that the cancer was back. We couldn't believe it. She had to undergo a stem cell transplant and has suffered some deficits."

"Oh no, Barbara," I said, devastated to hear her news. "Did Lyn have any new symptoms before that MRI?"

"No, nothing at all. She was afraid to tell you about her relapse because she thought it would scare you, Marie. I'll try to keep you informed."

She was right—it did scare me. In fact, I was petrified.

I never heard from Barbara again, but a few months later, I searched Lyn's name on the Internet, and found what I had hoped not to—her obituary in a Minneapolis newspaper. It ended with "after a courageous battle with primary central nervous system lymphoma."

Mine would probably read the same, but I desperately didn't want it to. I prayed for Lyn's soul and begged God to give me a second chance.

George, Age 79, from Colorado

The senior member of our online support group was a man named George from Colorado. Here, in his own words, is the story he posted an incredible sixteen years after his cancer diagnosis.

> One day in April, my wife Anne and I were out shopping. I pulled into the parking lot and found that my legs and arms wouldn't work properly. After I struggled to get into the store, I couldn't verbalize my

thoughts. By the time we got home, the episode had passed, but I was still weak and tired, unable to even pick up a bag of garden soil.

Shortly after that I developed double vision and went to see our eye doctor. She did hours of testing and then told me that something was pressing on my optic nerve and I needed an MRI right away. I had the brain scan on a Friday and got a call from my doctor the next day telling me to come in right away. I was told that I had four golf ball-sized tumors—three in the center of my brain and one in the left frontal lobe—and I needed a biopsy fast.

We returned home in a state of shock. When the pathology report came in, it confirmed primary central nervous system lymphoma. At this point, Anne had to feed me and help me dress. I was drooling and could not think straight. I prayed for help just to feel like a human being again. I was 64 years old and due to celebrate my 45th wedding anniversary, but the doctors predicted that I had only three months to live. Now my wife would be a widow and I would never see my grandchildren grow up. I asked our pastor and all of our friends and family to pray for me.

One night, a famous person who had recently died [Anne later told me it was the actor and later California Congressman Sonny Bono] visited me in a dream. He told me not to give up, that if I fought hard, I would survive. After months of treatment with chemotherapy and radiation, I went into remission, and here I am 16 years after a doctor told me I had three months to live.

George's story was pretty amazing, and it gave me more hope than anything I had heard so far.

Misery Loves Company

BARRY'S VIRTUAL SUPPORT group was a godsend to me in my journey, but I later found a bricks-and-mortar community of fellow cancer patients that became another resource through the battle.

Margie, a real estate agent from one of our Conway offices, called me one day to say she had read about my illness in the company newsletter. She told me about a place called The Wellness Community (now the Cancer Support Community of the South Shore) that held weekly meetings just twenty minutes from my house.

I called my friend Elaine, who had recently finished breast cancer treatments, and she agreed to go with me. Before we were allowed to attend the group support sessions, each of us had to go for an orientation meeting with the program director, Tim Cummings.

On a bleak midwinter morning, I dragged myself up the steps of the Wellness Community, feeling foggy-headed, and went into the director's office. Tim jumped up from his desk to greet me with an outstretched hand. He was an older man with shoulder-length salt-and-pepper hair and a white beard.

He was wearing an olive-green cotton shirt, with his sleeves rolled up to the elbows and khaki pants.

"Marie, please tell me your whole story," he said, settling back in his leather swivel chair. "Right from the beginning of your illness until now."

I told him my journey from the birth of Ben onward in a slightly manic, run-on manner ending with the morose statement—"Only 20 percent of people with my kind of brain tumor stay in remission longer than five years, so I'm pretty much screwed."

"Well you know something, Marie, there have to be some dots on that line of statistics that make up the 20 percent," he said. "And who's to say that you won't be one of them?"

I left our meeting feeling more hopeful than I had in a long while, and Elaine and I were invited to join the group session the next week. When we got there, we were escorted into a small room behind a closed door. There were seven people—six women and one man—sitting in a circle on beige fabric chairs and a coral couch. A glass lamp with the word "HOPE" sat on a square glass coffee table next to a supersized box of Kleenex. I wondered how long before the weeping would begin.

The first meeting of the support group did not go well for me. Tim went around the room and asked each person to report on their status and to give Elaine and me a brief overview of their condition since we were new to the community. Two of the women were emaciated, and one was on oxygen. But when it was their turn to speak, they were animated and upbeat even though the symptoms they were reporting made mine look like a stuffy nose. They were talking about feeding tubes, seizures, bleeding, and other details too graphic to repeat.

When it was my turn to talk, the people in the room seemed interested and offered some advice, but I didn't feel uplifted when I left there. Hearing other cancer patients discuss the painful details of their illnesses wasn't helping me.

"I'm not going back there again," I told Elaine as we were walking down the front stairs to the parking lot. "I didn't like it at all, did you?"

"I didn't love it, but I think you're being too impulsive. It was hard for us to hear all those people's sad stories, but we won't have to listen to that every week. It's just because we were new, and they had to give us their backgrounds. Let's try it one more time, and then if we still don't like it, we won't go back."

I took Elaine's advice, and the next session was better and the one after that even better.

We ended up going to the weekly support group for nearly two years. As time went by, I wanted to keep going, not only for what the members were giving me but for what I was able to give them, whether it was a piece of advice or just a few laughs.

"You are our comic relief, Marie," said Tim on many occasions. "Just keep telling us your crazy stories. That's your job." Of course, there were times when I had to reach for that big Kleenex box when talking about setbacks or impending test results. The people in my group were all grappling with battles of their own, but we laughed more at our meetings than we cried, and we came to develop lasting friendships. I wouldn't have missed my Wednesday afternoons at the Wellness Community for anything.

Lesson learned: Support groups are good. You need them. They need you.

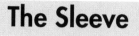

The Sleeve

DURING THE COURSE of my battle with PCNSL, the hellish, ever-present side effect of a buzzing and burning left arm was intermittently driving me to distraction. This symptom started on the day after my first steroid dose and worsened with every chemo treatment thereafter.

"It feels like someone has surgically implanted a buzz saw into my arm," I told a nurse one day while she was taking my blood pressure.

"Oh no, that didn't happen, Mrs. Fricker," she said. (Did she really think I was serious about the saw?) "The vibration is just a side effect of the steroids or your chemo."

And so the buzzing continued until one day when I stumbled upon something that was to be my salvation. It was a microwavable pillow that was shaped like a rectangle—about a foot long and five inches wide. It was filled with stones, had a flannel cover, and smelled like cinnamon. Someone had given it to Al to help his lower back pain, and he had never used it. I wondered if there was any chance that it might help me.

I came across this find in the bottom of a closet, zapped it for two minutes, and slipped my arm inside of its cover from hand to elbow. Amazingly, the buzz lessened and almost stopped. I had tried heated pillows before, but none had helped. I think this one was different because I could actually wear it, which is why I called it "the sleeve."

I took the sleeve everywhere I went, heating it up about six times a day and using it cold when I couldn't get to a microwave. Even just the weight of it soothed the pain, and every night I drifted off to sleep smelling the scent of warm cinnamon. I even took it to the hospital with me during my treatments because the chemo always intensified the buzzing.

On one fateful morning at the Brigham, however, the unthinkable happened. A nurse's aide had stripped the sheets off my bed with my sleeve inside of them. She then threw the linens down the laundry shoot, which apparently is equivalent to tossing something into the Bermuda Triangle, never to be seen again. I pleaded with my nurse to find it for me. "You don't understand," I said with tears streaming down my face. "It's the only thing that helps the buzzing."

Alarmed by my behavior, she said she would call housekeeping and see what could be done. A few hours later, the phone rang next to my bed. "Mrs. Fricker, we have not been able to find your pillow," said a woman with a nasally voice. "But the hospital will be happy to reimburse you for its cost."

I cried like Tom Hanks in the movie *Castaway* when his only "friend" on the island, the soccer ball that he had humanized and named Wilson, floated beyond his reach in the open sea. The sleeve was my Wilson, and although several microwavable pillows would follow it, none of them would ever take its place.

Journal entry:

On the way home from my treatment today, Al and I visited Alli's house. I held the baby for a long time in the rocking chair until he had explosive diarrhea through his diaper and onto my lap. I had read in one of my "God, don't do that!" coping with cancer books that you shouldn't come into contact with an infant's feces while getting chemotherapy, so I handed Ben off to Alli like a ticking time bomb.

She cleaned him up and put him in his swing from which he happily smiled and kicked his chubby legs for the rest of our visit.

Yes, I would be happy to accept the award as Grandmother of the Year.

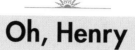

Oh, Henry

ONE MONTH AFTER the demise of the sleeve, I was back in the hospital for another treatment and feeling despondent. The little energy I'd had the day before was gone. That's what the chemo always did—it packed a wallop. But I looked at it this way—if it was just as hard on the tumors as it was on me, then maybe it was working.

I had no visitors all day or night, and I was lonely. I wished someone would pop in so that I could force myself to take a walk up and down the familiar halls of the oncology unit. To pass the time, I started watching fluids drip from my IV pole into the tube that led to my port. I had named the pole Henry after my father since it was my constant companion for four days and three nights every month.

My father had died from a heart attack when Alli was just a year old. It was in December of 1980, and I was talking on the phone with my sister-in-law Lorraine when an operator cut into the line with an emergency call. I heard a man's voice say, "This is Officer Sullivan of the Arlington Police Department, Mrs. Fricker. Please hang up the phone and call your mother. Your father has just passed away."

"What, what do you mean? My father is dead?" I started screaming, "What am I going to do? What am I going to do?"

"Do you need someone to come over there, Mrs. Fricker?"

"No," I said, hanging up on him and wiping water from my eyes so that I could make out the numbers on the phone as I called my mother. She answered on the first ring.

"Oh, Ree Ree [she was using my childhood name], your father is gone," she said with unexpected calmness in her voice. She was still in shock.

"Oh my god. What happened, Mom?"

"He woke up this morning and was sitting on the side of his bed. I asked him if he was okay, and he said, 'I'm just trying to psyche myself up to get dressed.' I helped him put his shirt on, and he took it right off again. I don't know how, but I knew it was the end. I hugged him and said, 'Remember our lovely girls, Henry?' He nodded his head, stood up, and just fell to the floor like a sack of clothes."

My father, a longtime bachelor who married late in life, was a bit of a loner. I never remember sitting on "daddy's lap" and hearing him say "I love you," but I knew he did. The warmest declaration I ever got from him was an occasional "Blessings on thee, daughter," as he tapped the top of my head with a grin while passing by me.

It was appropriate then that I should name my constant but untouchable IV companion in his honor. Flowing into me from pouches on Henry were drips of sodium bicarbonate and sodium chloride—sodium—all salt. No wonder I was blowing up like the Hindenburg. The fluids going into me necessitated frequent bathroom trips to flush them out, which were no easy tasks. I had to slide a white plastic "hat" with the name Fricker written on it in black magic marker under the toilet seat, pee in it, and then put it on the floor for a nurse to remove and analyze. I wouldn't want that job.

The distance from the toilet to the tiny sink was about three steps, but in my early days as an inpatient, I would sit there for twenty minutes with my head in my hands to summon the strength for the trip. And when I finally reached the destination, the left handle of the faucet inevitably unscrewed in my hand and fell to the floor. But as time went by, the bathroom routine got easier, and I rarely drew the short straw for the sink with the faulty faucet.

Journal entry:

It's so odd to see the trappings of Christmas on the streets of Boston while facing this horrible battle. How can twinkling lights and sleigh bells be a part of people's everyday lives when my private battle wages on in darkness? I shouldn't think this way because I know that Jesus is with me, and I should want to celebrate his birth and honor him. That's the way I should be thinking.

Ho Ho No

I WAS WAITING in the Dana-Farber clinic for another chemo treatment one week before Christmas. A few of the nurses were wearing Santa Claus hats, which was more depressing than festive in this atmosphere. A young man in a brown knit ski cap got called into the infusion room before me. Thin and weary looking, he trudged through the doors as my name was called, and I followed him in.

The walls in this area were wood-paneled with large framed prints of purple pansies here and there and one of a young girl riding a bike in a field. Most of the people would get their treatments in the clinic and then go on to their jobs or homes. A middle-aged man wearing a diamond pinkie ring and a dark blue suit was obviously heading back to the office after his infusion.

For me, it would take another three days for my high-dose drug to be drained from my system. The hospital stays were not fun, but I would rather have been there after getting these megaloads of methotrexate than at home, just in case something went wrong.

After my treatment, I was admitted to a room on the sixth floor of Brigham and Women's—my new home away from home. In tribute to the holiday season, the lobby was filled with homemade baked goods and crafts, and a male nurse was wearing an elf's hat with a white pompom attached to a spring on top of it. I wished they'd stop trying so hard to be merry around here.

Luckily, my favorite nurse, Donna, was on duty that night. Donna had grown up in South Boston and now lived in Quincy with her German shepherd, Beau.

"I always work the Thanksgiving and holiday shifts for the other nurses who have kids at home," she said. "The dog won't miss me that much."

Donna told me that her brother Dave had died of non-Hodgkin's lymphoma, but he had lived for eight quality years in remission before the cancer returned.

"I've seen some people with your illness who get better with the treatment and some who don't," she said. "I have no idea why the methotrexate works so well for some patients and not for others. Marie, you can't think about curing your lymphoma. Just think about treating it as a chronic illness for the rest of your life."

Even if that were true, I didn't want to hear it. I couldn't imagine having debilitating chemotherapy off and on for the rest of my life. I wanted to believe that I could be cured and that all this could end. But Donna was very kind and often sat with me in the night to calm my fears.

Lesson learned: Battling cancer is like nothing you have ever done in your life. Every cold you ever had, every flu, every abscessed tooth had a duration period and a point at which the suffering would be over. Cancer is a land of limbo. You never know when or if it will ever end.

Journal entry:

I read in one of my positive-thinking books that you should make a list of everything you're grateful for when you're going through tough times. So I scribbled out a gratitude list on the back of my hospital menu this morning.

I am grateful:

For Dr. Norden, who has now given me his e-mail address in case I need him quickly.

That I have not had nausea and vomiting during my chemo treatments.

For the support of my friends and family.

That I can see clearly again with no double vision.

That I can now walk without a walker or cane.

That my tumors are shrinking.

For the laptop computer that keeps me sane.

I don't feel any better, but maybe it's working subliminally.

Food for Thought

ANOTHER TIP I got from one of my cancer self-help books was to try to develop a "mind-body connection" to stimulate my immune system to attack my tumors. The author urged, "Select a strong symbol for your immune cells, such as a pack of hungry lions. Then envision your cancer as a pile of raw hamburger."

It was getting gross, but I kept reading.

"Now imagine the lions attacking the raw hamburger, gobbling it up, and digesting it until there is nothing left."

I was supposed to practice this mental exercise three times a day for thirty minutes at a time. The book said to meditate in the most relaxing place you know, so I drove to my beloved lighthouse for the sessions. The problem was that no matter how soothing it was to be in my favorite place looking out at the sea, imagining bloodthirsty lions ripping apart my brain just wasn't doing it for me. After a couple of unsuccessful attempts, I decided to forget the mind-body connection and connect with Rod Stewart on my CD player instead.

My next stab at "mindfulness meditation" came from another of my cancer manuals. The writer said to put three raisins on a table and observe them for two whole minutes.

(I mean seriously, what was there to observe? They were just sitting there.) I was then supposed to put the raisins in my mouth and eat them while noticing exactly how I was chewing and swallowing each one.

"Knowing what you are doing while you are doing it is the essence of mindfulness," wrote the author.

Huh?

"You'll never learn to meditate," said Al. "You can't stop talking long enough to do it." He had a point.

"You're Getting Drowsy..."

SINCE MEDITATION DIDN'T seem to be my thing, someone in my support group suggested that I go to see a counselor who specializes in helping people with cancer. She gave me the name of a local therapist named Mary Beth, and I booked an appointment. Al drove me there and waited in the parking lot during the thirty-minute session.

Mary Beth was an attractive blonde who looked to be in her early forties but told me she was a sixty-two-year-old widow. Like a good friend, she listened to my woes, commiserated, and made some suggestions. I really don't remember much about my sessions with this woman because I was so out of it when I went to her, but I know she was nice and made me feel better. She also told me about her favorite guided meditation CD called *Your Present: A Half-Hour of Peace*. I bought it from Amazon and gave it a try. It was much better than the lions or the raisins.

Another member of my cancer support group suggested the next practitioner on my journey of alternative therapies.

"Have you thought of going to a hypnotist?" asked Valerie, who was "positively thinking" her way through melanoma. "I think it might help you manage your pain and maybe even give you a more hopeful attitude." (Obviously I was more of a downer to the group than I had thought.)

She recommended a local hypnotist named Amanda, who had helped Valerie's husband to quit smoking. When I called the office to set up an appointment, Amanda asked what my needs were. I told her I had a rare brain tumor and wanted help with two things—paying less attention to the pain and buzzing in my arm and believing that I would be cured.

"Well, I'm sure you already have enough medical bills to deal with, so your first two sessions will be free," she said. "This is something I like to do for people who are ill."

Wow. That wasn't expected. I knew her regular rate was $125 an hour, so this was a big perk. I drove to her office the next day and waited in a small room filled with magazine racks until my name was called. Amanda greeted me with a warm smile. She had wavy brown shoulder-length hair and strikingly blue eyes. She ushered me into her office and told me to sit in a hard-backed chair.

"Are you a woman of faith, Marie?" she asked.

I told her I was a Catholic but not a very strict one. I noticed that a bin by her desk was overflowing with crushed cigarette packs—the residuals of "Kick the Habit" sessions she had held for individuals and groups.

The first thing she did was give me a chain with a crystal attached to it.

"Now I want you to make the chain swing in a particular direction just by the power of your will," she said. "People who are spiritual can do this very easily, and those who aren't can't make it move at all. Now try to make the chain go back and forth, then in a circle, and then stop."

I concentrated, and the crystal obliged immediately. I swear I never consciously moved the chain.

"You are extremely spiritual," said Amanda. "Now let's get to the hypnosis session. She moved me over to a thickly padded reclining chair and lowered the lights in the room. She touched my forehead and counted back from three.

"I am asking Jesus and his mother to be with us, and they are here now," she said. "The buzzing in your arm is no longer going to interfere with your enjoyment of life. You will be able to go about your business free of worry about the constant vibration. In fact, you will find a way to lessen it gradually just as you would turn down the volume on a radio, and it will no longer upset you."

Then she told me something that sent a chill up my spine. "Marie, God called you by name when he gave you this cancer," she said. "You are one of the chosen few who are destined to help others, and it was necessary for you to experience this depth of suffering to motivate you to help other people who are suffering too."

This really hit home with me because in the first few weeks of my illness, a single thought kept recurring in my mind: if I get better, I need to help others who are as scared and sick as I am now. I had even told Al and the kids about it at the time.

The next segment of the hypnosis session was quite unexpected. I had no idea I was so popular among dead people—even dead people I never knew. But according to Amanda, I was the life of the party that day in her office. Evidently there was a father-figure spirit who kept calling me his "sweet baby girl." Henry Gallishaw would have choked on that term of endearment, but then maybe death had mellowed him. There was also a motherly spirit, described by Amanda as a thin, gray-haired woman. Unless my portly mom had met Dr. Atkins in the afterlife and shed fifty pounds on his diet, I had no idea who this person was. But according to my hypnotist, these two parental ghosts were very much concerned about my well-being and were "constantly hovering over" me. Hey, I'd take all the help I could get.

After their arrival came many others, and with each one's emergence, Amanda would describe the new celestial guest and ask me if I knew who he or she was. I made a few guesses but wasn't really sure of any of them. "I see a young man now, bald head, very thin, just passed from an illness," she said. "Do you know him?"

"Well, my next-door neighbor Chris lost her nephew Jimmy to cancer about a month ago," I said.

"Yes, this is Jimmy, and he wants you to bring a message to his aunt. Tell her that he says 'thank you' for what she did and that he is at peace."

I promised to deliver the message.

The next visitor was a middle-aged woman with curly hair followed by an old man with horn-rimmed glasses. It was really getting crowded in here. Despite my hypnotic state, I was tiring of this "name that spirit" game and wanted it to end.

"I really don't know any more deceased people," I said. "I've used them all up." I came from a very small family and had run dry of dead relatives and friends.

Amanda suddenly began counting backward from ten.

"Ten, nine, eight…You will be fully alert when I reach the number one."

I didn't have the heart to tell her that I had been fully alert the entire time.

"Don't worry if you think you didn't go under," she said. "Your mind absorbed what I was telling you at the level it was supposed to. For the next ten days, I want you to repeat this ten times before you go to sleep—'Every day in every way, I'm getting better and better.'"

I walked back down the stone steps from Amanda's office feeling relaxed but knowing that I had not been hypnotized.

Evil Spirits

THE NEXT MORNING, I made a phone call to my neighbor Chris and delivered the thank-you message from her deceased nephew. She immediately burst into tears. "Oh, Marie, you have no idea how much this call means to me," she said. "I have been feeling horrible about Jimmy, and to hear that he is at peace is incredible. I think I may sleep tonight for the first time in six weeks."

I was genuinely happy that something good had come from my hypnosis session, at least for somebody. As I started brushing my teeth at the sink, I noticed the familiar buzzing in my left arm, but only for a minute or two. My agenda for the day was empty (what else was new?), so after I took a shower and got dressed, I drove to the lighthouse, where I would kill a few hours watching the world around me.

This place never failed to bring me peace. Al and I had gone to this spot every Sunday morning since we moved to town in 1987. We would sit in the car drinking our Dunkin' Donuts coffees and observe what we called the rear-window (named for our favorite Hitchcock movie) scenes that played out in front of us. The area was always alive with boats coming and going, and you could see the white-steepled church, fishing pier, harbor shops, and restaurants on the other side of the water.

Today was no different. A young family with a baby in a backpack was walking to the end of the stone jetty and back. Shiny black labs chased sticks thrown into the water as seagulls circled close to the cars hoping for scraps tossed from open windows. A flock of black sea terns flew in perfect unison in one direction and then the other as if trying to decide which way to go against a cloudless sky. An old couple strolled hand in hand and sat on one of the wooden benches to look out at the sea.

After a while a big red SUV pulled up and unloaded kids, dogs, and fishing poles. In front of the lighthouse, a young couple wearing bike helmets was studying the bulletin board that held faded newspaper articles about the *Etrusco*, a ship that had run aground on Scituate's shore in the mid-1900s. Al and I always laughed at this sight because the yellowed stories in the Plexiglas-covered stand hadn't been changed in sixteen years, and yet the tourists still seemed to eat them up.

With more than enough rear-window scenes to satisfy me, I drove home to let Otis out and feed him. Then I picked Brenda up, and we went to Kohl's to buy a new nightgown for the hospital. When I looked at my watch inside the changing room, it was 4:00 p.m., and I realized I hadn't even thought about my buzzing arm all day. Had it been hurting less than usual, or was I just too busy to notice it? Could the relief have come from the hypnosis session the day before? Just in case, I booked another appointment immediately.

Unfortunately, this one didn't go as well. Amanda spent the entire session waving something called dowsing rods around me to expel dark spirits from my body, which she said were contributing to my illness. At the end of the procedure, she declared me "clean," but the whole thing really gave me the creeps, and I didn't go back again. I wanted to be hypnotized, not exorcised.

Still, I got some laughs at the support group when I retold my experience waving a plastic straw in the air and chanting "Evil spirit, be gone!" But the truth is that after that first hypnosis session, the buzzing in my arm did get better, and the relief lasted for quite a while. Coincidence or consequence, I guess I'll never know.

Lesson learned: Try the alternative therapies even if you're skeptical. If they work, you're golden, and if not, at least you have a good story for the group.

A Bad Day Gets Better

My hospital stay in February, one day postchemo, started out badly. The usual stuff was worse—shortness of breath, chest pressure, buzzing, and lethargy. My daily journal entry had just four words—*yikes, this is tough.*

But then came my saviors: Alli and Jay arrived in the midst of an afternoon snowstorm. "Hi, Mom. The baby was crying all morning, so I got sprung to visit you," said my daughter with a smile. "Let's go down to the Au Bon Pain and get some food. I'm starving."

"Hop in this wheelchair, Ma," said Jay as Alli pushed my IV pole to the elevator that brought us to the lobby. I wondered if the sight of me and my paraphernalia would ruin people's appetites in the Au Bon Pain checkout line, but a bandage-wrapped mummy of a man on crutches was ordering a Coke in front of me, and no one gave either of us a second glance. I guess in this atmosphere the walking wounded were the norm.

With my usual ravenous appetite, I couldn't decide between pea soup and chicken noodle, so I ordered them both, along with a blond brownie. And then we actually walked around the hospital gift shop, where I bought a Red Sox bib for Ben.

When the kids left, I settled back into my room for the night, feeling so much better.

Journal entry:

> A Eucharistic minister came into my room this morning to bring me communion. She was a stick-thin Bohemian-looking older lady with a white bob hairdo and a big silver charm around her neck that said, "BELIEVE." She held my hand in her ice-cold ones and said a prayer for healing from the Bible. She kept referring to me as "my sister, Marie," which for some strange reason was comforting. She was a rather odd messenger for the Catholic Church, but I liked her.

Looking Out for Number 1

AFTER MANY MONTHS of inpatient stays at the hospital, I realized that I had to be my own advocate because sometimes mistakes did happen. I had previously trusted that doctors and nurses were infallible, but minor glitches were occurring, and I had learned to watch out for them. During one of the times when I was roommates with Mary, I looked up at my IV pole to see a pouch of liquid that had her name and not mine written on it.

Panicked, I pressed the red call button, and a nurse arrived. She was a woman I didn't know, and she spoke in a hushed whisper. "Don't be alarmed, Mrs. Fricker. You're getting the correct drug," she said. "Your bottle didn't come up from the pharmacy, so we are just using one of your roommate's. It's exactly the same medicine. Would you like a Xanax?"

I came to realize that whenever I showed concern about any practice or procedure that seemed suspicious, I was offered a tranquilizer. I guess "What is Xanax?" was the answer to every *Jeopardy* question ever asked in this strange new world.

The next day, I never received my morning medications and had to ask for them. The nurse said something about a paper being stuck to some other paper and told me she was sorry.

Lesson learned: Be your own advocate. Don't assume that everything is right because sometimes it isn't. And if all else fails, take a Xanax.

Journal entry:

Every morning when I first open my eyes, I feel normal for a minute or two. There is no arm or head buzzing because of a night of nonmovement and no weakness because I'm lying down. And then I remember what I'm going through, that I will have to haul my sorry ass out of bed and grope my way through the rest of the day in a fog that never lifts.

The actor Christopher Reeve, who became a paraplegic after falling from a horse, wrote in his autobiography *Still Me* that when he dreamed at night, he was always the pre-accident him—running and hiking and acting in movies. Then he'd wake up and realize that he was paralyzed and connected to a breathing tube, and it would hit him like a sledgehammer all over again. That passage in his book had always disturbed me, but now it hit closer to home.

Bitter — Party of One

A NEW EMOTIONAL syndrome that I will refer to as health envy set in not long after my cancer diagnosis, and it persisted for a long time. I would look at other people walking by me on the streets and going about their business in the real world and be extremely jealous of them.

"Look at those old ladies in there," I said to my sister one morning when we drove by a Dunkin' Donuts where about six white-haired women were sitting by the window laughing and eating bagels. "I'm at least twenty years younger than any person in that group, and yet I can barely move. I kind of hate them."

"Oh, cut it out, Ree. You don't mean that. But I can sort of understand how you feel, and I would probably be feeling the same way in your shoes."

Betty and I had the "got your back" kind of relationship that no matter how off-the-wall one sister's thoughts might be at a particular time, the other would justify the feeling in some small measure to make the "crazy" sibling feel better. I knew she was trying to do that now, but it wasn't helping.

I sat in a parking space in front of the Dunkin' Donuts window while Betty went in to buy me a coffee. Unfortunately, this gave me a front-row seat to the fun and frivolity that was going on inside with this group of senior friends. One woman with hair like white cotton candy suddenly threw her head back laughing while her companions followed suit. All I could imagine was that these people probably had a good fifteen or twenty years of life ahead of them. They had normal brains, ones that if scanned in an MRI machine would show no white spots that lit up like lanterns after getting injected with contrast dye. Hell, they wouldn't even know what contrast dye was.

I didn't wish my prognosis on any of them, but I was bitter, and I wasn't proud of it.

The Ostrich Syndrome

WHEN MY COMPANY'S short-term disability policy ran out during my illness, I had to apply for extended benefits through the State Disability Commission. I was asked to obtain all the medical records related to my brain tumor in order to qualify, so I requested them in writing.

A few weeks later, Betty and I were having lunch at my house when I received a thick package in the mail. According to a cover letter, it included lab reports, pathology results, scans, and discharge summaries dating back to my first ER visit. The reporter in me wanted desperately to read and learn every fact contained in these documents, but the pessimist in me was afraid to read a word of it. What if some statement in these papers shattered any hopes I had of a cure? Maybe Dr. Norden wasn't telling me everything because he knew I couldn't handle it.

Stealing a quick glance at the pathology report, I saw the diagnosis: Large B-cell non-Hodgkin's Lymphoma and then a horrifying word—*staging*. I looked away immediately. I had never asked Dr. Norden what stage my tumors were in because I was too afraid to find out. If they were Stage III or IV, I would be terrified, so I was better off not knowing.

Still, I didn't want to follow in my mother's ostrich-like footsteps about her breast cancer. Mom never answered any phone calls from the hospital and wouldn't read any doctor's letters that came to the house. Out of fear, she dragged her feet every step of the way, and maybe things would have been different if she hadn't.

"You read it for me," I said, handing the papers to my sister. "But don't tell me if there's anything in it that would scare me."

"Well that's a no-win situation for me," said Betty. "If I read it and say nothing, you'll think there's something terrible in there. So unless I find something good to tell you, I'm basically screwed. Therefore, I am not going to read it."

She had a point. I decided to buck up and look at the report myself. I ended up reading all of it, but it turned out that nothing was written next to the word *staging*. I later found out that PCNSL is not staged like other cancers because it's confined to the brain and doesn't spread to other parts of the body. You'd think that would be a good thing, but of course, it isn't. Cancer in the brain is enough to kill you all by itself.

Lesson learned: You may want to pull an ostrich act and hide your head in the sand, but it's better to know the truth unless you really can't handle it. You may be stronger than you think.

Nuts?

I'M NOT SURE if all people who have been afflicted with "an insult to the brain," as my son, the paramedic, refers to my brain tumor, are inclined to doubt their sanity, but I did, particularly on one occasion. It was a Monday morning, shortly after a chemo treatment, and I was feeling pretty out of it.

Alli had called me the night before to say that Debbie, one of the graphic designers in my office, had written on her Facebook page that her sister-in-law Jean had died of an aneurism. I knew Debbie must be devastated because she was very close to Jean, so I called her at work to offer my condolences.

Maureen, the headquarters receptionist, answered the phone in her brusque but good-natured manner. "Jack Conway Company," she said. "Can I help you?"

"Hi, Maureen, it's Marie. Is Debbie in? I heard about her sister-in-law's death."

"What are you talking about, honey?" said Maureen, "Debbie didn't have any loss in her family. You must have dreamt it."

I hung up the phone in terror.

I tried the affirmation—"Every day in every way I'm getting better and better." It didn't work.

"Oh my god, I don't know the difference between reality and a dream anymore," I said to Al, who was carving up his usual fruit bowl quantity of apples, oranges, cantaloupe, and grapes for breakfast. "I could have sworn that Alli told me that Debbie's sister-in-law had died.

"Don't worry about it, Ree," he said. "You're just a little confused."

I was more than confused; I was probably brain-damaged from either the tumor or the chemo, and I could no longer trust my own thoughts. I prepared to wallow on the couch for the day when the phone rang. It was Kelly calling from the office.

"Just checking in on you, lady," she said with a laugh. "How are you?"

"I'm doing okay," I said. And then, almost afraid to ask, I added "Is there anything new at Conway?"

Kelly's voice lowered to a whisper. "I wasn't going to tell you this, but Debbie's sister-in-law Jean just passed away," she said. "She had an aneurism. Isn't that horrible?"

"Oh, thank God," I said, flooded with relief.

"What do you mean?" asked Kelly with fear in her voice.

"No, not about Jean's death. I'm just so glad I'm not crazy."

"Okay then, well, I'll call you later."

She must have thought I had lost my mind, but I knew I hadn't—at least not yet.

Journal entry:

If somebody asks me what I want to do today, my answer is to curl up in a ball and pull the covers over my head until tomorrow. I honestly don't think

I can take feeling like this for one more minute of one more day. When I saw Dr. Norden yesterday, I asked him when I would start to feel better. He put his arm around me and said, "Marie, you probably aren't going to feel good for the next year or so, but remember we're trying to cure a tumor here." I would be devastated right now, but he did say the word *cure*.

Sammy Sends Help

JUST TWO MONTHS before I was diagnosed with a brain tumor, my nine-year-old black pug Sammy died of a brain tumor (yeah, some coincidence). I have loved a lot of dogs in my life, but this one was my soul mate. When the kids grew up and moved out, he sort of took their place, nuzzling under my arm in an upright position like a person and watching TV with me. His soulful brown eyes followed my every move, and his unconditional adoration did much to ease the pain of my unwanted empty nest.

And then one day, Jay called me at work to say that Sammy was having a seizure. Less than a month later, he died in my arms in the same spot the two of us had always shared on the couch. I cried for weeks and vowed never to love another dog.

"Mom, I'm going to adopt a Boston terrier," said Jay as he was sitting at the computer at my rolltop desk about three months after my diagnosis. "There's a breeder who's giving away a five-year-old female named Maxine. I just e-mailed her."

The woman wrote back immediately and told him to meet her at a shopping mall fifty miles away. "Come with me, Ma," he said. "It will be good for you to get out."

I was nervous about going because a snowstorm was brewing. But then again, what did I have to lose? Better to die in a car crash than from a brain tumor, so I went out to the driveway and got into Jay's white GMC truck, and we drove to the parking lot of the Swansea Mall.

Jay looked for a red van with a Boston terrier sticker on the back window and found it right away. We pulled in next to it, and a heavyset woman wearing a puffy fur-hooded parka got out with a small black-and-white beauty in her arms. Her face looked familiar, and I suddenly realized that I had met her before.

"Is your name Shirley?" I asked, almost not believing my own eyes.

"Yes, it is," she said, looking a little surprised. This lady was the breeder who had sold me my Sammy from a litter of black pugs in Rhode Island almost ten years earlier. Loving this dog the way I did, I had tried many times to find Shirley to buy another puppy from the same bloodline, but I could never track her down. Her number had been disconnected, and a cousin with the same last name that I found through Superpages told me he hadn't seen or heard from her in years.

I had been so bummed, but now here she was, standing in a parking lot during a blizzard, handing me another dog. In my foggy mind, it made total sense. Sammy knew I needed him during this desperate time in my life, and he was sending a pinch hitter.

This "free" Boston terrier ended up costing Jay $600 to treat a uterine infection and a severe case of hookworms. Shirley had told us that Maxine had been bred only once and had lived in a kennel all her life. But we got a different story when we took her to our vet for an exam.

"I see evidence of at least four botched C-sections in this dog," said Dr. T, pointing to an ultrasound on a monitor in her office. "Her uterus is almost fused to her bladder, but I think we can fix her up."

Maxine's personality was borderline catatonic (she barely moved from any spot in which you placed her), but she was loving and sweet, and her face reminded me of a lot of my soul mate. Jay was hunting for an apartment that allowed pets, and he asked me to keep her at my house until he found one.

"Are you crazy?" I said. "How can I take care of another animal at a time like this?" But what I didn't know then was that this animal would take care of me. In the many months that followed, every time I would return home weak and spent from a chemo treatment, I would slump into my glider and haul Maxine into my lap. She would lay with her head on my shoulder until it all felt better.

I recently read a book called *God Winks*. Its premise is that when uncanny coincidences happen in your life, God is sending you a message. This one was from Sammy.

Not on This Parade!

I WAS SITTING in my hospital bed after my fourth chemo treatment waiting for the results of my latest MRI when Dr. Norden walked into the room. My stomach tightened but relaxed immediately when he put his right thumb up in the air.

"I have great news! Your lymphoma is in total radiological remission," he said jubilantly. "There's not a trace of the tumors on your scans. That doesn't necessarily mean that it's gone for good, Marie, but you are officially in remission. We're going to continue your chemo treatments for one more year with an MRI every other month."

The odds of PCNSL recurring were about 80 percent, but I wouldn't let myself think about that right now. The tumors were gone, and I was ecstatic. When Dr. Norden left, I called about ten people to share the news. They all cheered, and for the first time since the diagnosis, I felt hopeful.

Later that day, the on-call doctor came in my room to check on me.

"Did you hear that my MRI was clear?" I said to Dr. Buzz Killer. "I am so excited."

"Well, Mrs. Fricker, I wouldn't jump the gun here," he said. "You're in radiological remission, but we don't know how long that will last."

I thought about Victor, the nurse who had ruined my first bit of good news when the tumors were shrinking, and I wasn't about to let that happen again.

"Doctor, all I'm asking you is this. Without thinking about next week, next month, or next year, would it be accurate for me to say that today I do not have cancer?

"Well, yes."

That was all I needed. I was cancer-free, maybe not forever, but for now, and I was incredibly happy.

Lost in Familiar Places

ONE NIGHT, SHORTLY after I started driving again, I decided to go to Stop & Shop on my own and get some groceries. "I'll go with you, Ree," said Al, starting to put on his jacket.

"No, I have to do this myself," I said as I headed out for the market. It was two days after a chemo treatment, so my head was pretty spacey. But since this was apparently going to be my "new normal" for the foreseeable future, I figured I might as well accept it and trudge ahead.

I got to the store, picked out the food in each aisle, paid for it at the register, and then pushed my cart out into the parking lot. That's when it happened. I suddenly realized that nothing around me looked the least bit familiar. I didn't recognize the big yellow house across the street from the market, and my car was in a completely different spot than I remembered.

This must have been what that doctor was talking about in the Chief's Rounds when he asked if I had ever gotten lost in familiar places. I was terrified, but instead of letting the fear paralyze me, I decided to put my groceries in the car because that's what normal people do when they leave a supermarket. I refused to look left or right or think about being lost until all the food was in the trunk.

When the last bag went in, I summoned the courage to glance around me, and my brain fog began to lift like a fuzzy Polaroid picture coming slowly into focus. I realized where I was—not at the Stop & Shop that I usually went to in Cohasset but at the one in Norwell, down the street from my Conway office.

My legs were shaking as I got into my car and drove home. I called Dr. Norden immediately. "I'm in trouble," I said, relating the details of the supermarket fugue. "Do you think the chemo has affected my brain, or is the tumor back again? Should I get an MRI?"

"Don't worry, Marie. I'm not at all concerned," he said. "That kind of episode could happen to anyone. You usually go to the other store and had assumed that's where you were when you came out to the parking lot. Then when anxiety set in, you couldn't think straight. The methotrexate could be a contributing factor here, but I'm really not concerned about this."

I was still afraid, but I couldn't dwell on it. It would paralyze me to think that the tumor was back or that I had brain damage and wouldn't be able to do something as simple as going to a supermarket. It was time to think positively.

Every day in every way, I'm getting better and better.

Please God, let me believe it.

Journal entry:

I'm starting to rebound a little faster from my chemo treatments. They don't pack quite the punch that they used to, and I'm beginning to feel a little more like me. Hope it's not just wishful thinking.

A Twitch in Time

IT HAD BEEN several months since my tumors had disappeared from my MRI, and subsequent scans continued to show no trace of them.

"The longer you can stay in remission, the better your chances are of staying that way," said Dr. Norden, who would give me the smiling thumbs-up every other month after reading my MRI results. Despite the continued good news, I was always afraid when I first caught sight of his white coat in the doorway when he came to deliver the report of my latest scan.

As time passed, I seemed to be able to tolerate the chemo much better and was living a more normal life, going to movies, and visiting friends and family.

One night, Al and I were watching TV at Alli and Jeremy's house when I felt a weird twitching on one side of my face. I rubbed my cheek to make it go away, but it persisted. I ran into the bathroom to look in the mirror, and I could see the spasm happening again and again on the right side of my face.

"Alli, come in here quick," I yelled into the living room. "Look at my face."

"What? That twitching?" she said, touching my cheek. "That's just a nerve. I've had that before. Put something cold on it and see if it stops."

She brought me a small bag of frozen peas, and I held it against my face and looked in the mirror again. The spasm persisted for a few more minutes but then went away. I decided to send Dr. Norden an e-mail about the incident anyway. I expected his usual quick response—"Don't worry, Marie. I'm not concerned"—but what I got instead was a cell phone call from him within five minutes of sending the message.

"Hi, Marie, it's Andrew Norden," he said. "Listen, I don't want you to panic because it's probably not related to your lymphoma, but I'd like you to come in for an MRI tomorrow."

The adrenalin of anxiety began its familiar rush inside my body. "What do you mean? You think it's back, don't you? Oh my god, I'm screwed."

"No, I don't," he said in a calm tone. "I just want to be on the safe side."

But I knew he was worried. I left Alli's house convinced I was having a recurrence. The only MRI that I was able to schedule took place at ten the following night at the Dana-Farber. Al drove me over there, and I entered the dark tube, more frightened than ever about the outcome.

I had just gotten out of the scanner and was waiting for my IV line to be disconnected from my chest when a nurse handed me a telephone. "Mrs. Fricker, it's Dr. Norden. He wants to speak with you."

I couldn't believe it. I was still sitting on a gurney and hadn't even gotten dressed yet. How could he know anything so soon?

"Hi, Marie. It's Andrew," he said (he refers to himself by his first name even though I insist on calling him Dr. Norden to keep him on an older, authoritative plane). "Your MRI looks fine. The twitching was not related to your lymphoma. Go home now and get some sleep."

"You are amazing," I said, flooded with relief. "How did you get the results so quickly?"

"I had the radiologist send me the report electronically, and I read it from home. I knew you would worry all night if you didn't hear from me."

"Thank you so much for doing that. You are the best," I said.

"It was my pleasure."

Lesson learned: If you get a new symptom, don't assume it will go away. Tell your doctor. If you find out it's nothing, you won't worry all night.

Hero Worship

IN THE COURSE of my battle with brain cancer, one thing became increasingly clear. I admired, depended on, and absolutely worshipped the man who was trying so hard to save my life—Dr. Andrew Norden.

Doogie Howser or not, this guy was the real thing. He was as humble as he was brilliant, and he appreciated my weird sense of humor. He just seemed to get me from day 1, and he always knew how to diffuse a crisis—real or perceived.

"Dr. Norden, you're my hero," I said to him on the day he told me that my scans were clear.

"Yeah, right. If that tumor comes back, you'd be out of here in a heartbeat and leave me in the dust."

"That's not true," I said, not 100 percent sure that it wasn't. He knew me too well.

After one of my office visits, I asked Dr. Norden if I could interview him for the book I was hoping to write about my illness. "Sure," he said, probably thinking that it would never actually happen.

I met him in his office on a Wednesday afternoon with my rectangular reporter's notebook in hand and took notes as he answered my questions.

"So where do we begin?" he asked a little nervously.

"At the beginning. Where were you born and brought up, Dr. Norden?"

"In Baltimore, Maryland," he said. "I am the oldest of three sons. My parents' names were Roger and Jacqueline, and my dad worked in the medical imaging business. You're not going to have my fifth grade teacher pop out of a closet right now and say, 'Andrew Norden, this is your life,' are you?"

"Ha-ha, no, but that might have been a good idea," I said. "So are you married?"

"Yes. My wife's name is Pamela. She's a dermatologist. And we have two phenomenal little boys."

"Let's talk a little more about your academic background," I said. "As smart as you are, you had to be the valedictorian of your high school class, right?"

"Well, yes. But so was just about everyone I work with here," he said in his usual self-deprecating way.

"We are not talking about anyone else in this interview. This is all about you, as uncomfortable as that seems to make you."

He laughed.

"How did you first get interested in the area of neurology?"

"It started back in my eighth grade biology class when we got to the study of the brain. I found it absolutely fascinating, and I still do."

"Thank God for that! So where did you get your medical degrees?"

"At Brown University in Rhode Island and Yale Medical School."

"Wow. Pretty impressive. Did you graduate with honors?"

"Yes, but most people did."

"Don't start that again. We're talking about you, here. Would you mind if I asked what your cumulative average was at both schools because I'm guessing it was probably a perfect 4.0. Am I right?"

"Well, yes."

"Okay, so I'm in the presence of a genius just as I surmised. And how did you decide to become a neuro-oncologist?"

"When I went to Yale, I thought I was going to be a brain surgeon. But I decided neurology would be better because it would give me more personal contact with patients. I took care of a handful of brain cancer patients when I was a resident here at Brigham and Women's and Mass General for four years, and I felt drawn to them. They were people who were very sick and needed help."

"Many of your current patients are terminally ill with brain tumors that cannot be cured. How do you put your work aside and enjoy your life at home with so much sadness on the job?"

"If I spent all of my evenings thinking about what my patients are going through, I would never get to sleep," he said. "I hate to say that I have to remove myself from it, but I do. But there are times I can't put it aside, especially when I'm treating people who have young kids. A lot of my patients are in their twenties, thirties, and forties."

"I guess you're not losing any sleep over a fifty-five-year-old then, huh?"

"Ha-ha. I actually like getting the rare PCNSL patients like yourself because I have a better chance of helping them. I guess you could say that if you have to get a malignant brain tumor, your kind is the best one to have because it is so treatable and sometimes even curable."

"How often is it curable?" I asked, already knowing the answer.

"Marie, we've talked about this before," he said. "About 20 percent of the time."

"I know. I was just hoping you might want to change your answer. So there's word on the street that at the ripe old age of thirty-three, you just got a big promotion. I read that you have been chosen to head all of Dana-Farber's satellite cancer centers throughout the state. Can this possibly be true?"

"Yes, I'm very honored and excited about it."

"Now this new assignment isn't going to mean that you won't be able to see as many patients here anymore, is it? You can't desert me."

"Don't worry, I won't," he said. "The truth is I will be cutting back my days here at Dana-Farber a bit, but I'll always see my favorite patient."

I almost cried to think that he could make that statement after all I had put him through—constantly begging, "Please don't let me die," and asking, "Why am I not feeling better? When will the buzzing stop? Will I ever be me again? Will the tumors come back? Will my grandson remember me?"

We ended our little interview session with a hug as I went out into the hallway to join my son.

"You know, Jay," I said. "Dealing with me would have wiped the smile off almost anyone's face, but not Dr. Norden's."

"Yeah, no kidding. I had actually been thinking of going to medical school, but not anymore," said Jay. "If I had a patient like you, I'd have to kill myself. I don't know how he stands you."

Well, not only did Dr. Andrew Norden stand me, but he stood by me through the toughest trial of my life, and somehow, against all odds, he is still smiling.

Better

ABOUT TEN DAYS after chemo treatment number 7, something wonderful happened—I felt like me, not the precancer me but the me who had the guts to drive a car on the highway, socialize with others, and stay up with Al and watch *Saturday Night Live*. I was able to walk for ten minutes on a treadmill and, most importantly, to love, beyond all measure, my precious grandchild Ben. I was no longer afraid to pick the baby up, hold him, give him a bottle, or even change his diaper. Whenever Alli was at my house, I was always at his side.

He became the carrot that urged this donkey to go on, and if I won the battle of PCNSL, Benjamin James Kieffner was the prize.

Lesson learned: No matter how much you think that you will never feel better, wait it out. You will.

Journal entry:

I wrote a poem about the baby today.

Ben Smiles
Dealing with cancer can be a rough ride.
With chemo and nausea and losing my stride
Sometimes I think I can't go one more mile.

And then...Ben smiles.
His cheeks are bright pink with a dimple in one.
Two teeth on the bottom have just cut the gums.
The dark days of winter when all this began
Were brightened because of this new little man.
Hospitals, brain scans, and waiting for news
Battling symptoms and weakness and blues
Sometimes I think I can't handle these trials
And then...Ben smiles.

Belated Thanks

CHRISTOPHER, A NEW member of my online PCNSL support site, posted something one day that was a huge wake-up call to me. He was a forty-year-old guy from Alabama who had been feeling extremely weak and tired for several weeks but never went to see a doctor, just figuring that it would pass. One day, his wife, Lana, noticed that he was dragging his left foot and that the left side of his mouth was drooping.

Thinking he was having a stroke, she rushed him to the hospital, where he got an MRI that detected a lesion on his brain. He was mistakenly diagnosed with multiple sclerosis, just as I had been, but unlike me, he was not lucky enough to get the blunt but brilliant Dr. Wilson, who refused to treat me with steroids because he suspected a brain tumor.

Christopher's neurologist accepted the MS diagnosis and treated him with intravenous steroids for more than five months. After each dose, the tumors would shrink, but the symptoms would come back with a vengeance a short while later.

"The steroids were actually masking my husband's tumor," said Lana in a post to our group. "Sometimes it even disappeared, and Chris would get better and then decline again. This roller-coaster ride went on from September through January, and then I demanded a second opinion at a major hospital. After a biopsy, he was eventually diagnosed with primary central nervous system lymphoma. Today, after six months of chemo, he is in remission but remains partially paralyzed on his left side. I can't help feeling he would be doing much better now if not for the damage done by his first neurologist."

That statement hit home with me in a big way. Oh my god. I didn't just owe my life to the saintly Dr. Norden but also to the no-nonsense Dr. Wilson, who had refused my pleas for steroids, saying, "I will not treat you for something until I know what it is." Yes, there was another hero in this equation, perhaps a less lovable one, but a hero nonetheless, and he deserved my gratitude.

I called Dr. Wilson's office in Boston and asked to speak with him. His nurse said he was with a patient and would call me back. Unfortunately, I didn't realize that I had turned the ringer off on my cell phone and never heard three missed calls from him. Luckily, I saw a voice mail blinking and listened to it immediately.

"Mrs. Fricker, this is the last time I'm going to try to return your call. (There was that edge again.) I am leaving on vacation, so if you want to speak with me, you will have to contact me within ten minutes."

I dialed him back, and he answered on the first ring. "Dr. Wilson, I'm calling to offer you a sincere apology," I said before he could mention the missed calls. "You were absolutely right not to give me the steroids on the day I came to your office a year ago even though I begged you for them. Your opinion about the lesions on my brain being lymphoma was right long before a biopsy could confirm it. I'm in remission now, but who knows where I'd be if you had given me those drugs. You may have saved my life, and I am eternally grateful to you."

"Mrs. Fricker, your phone call has made my day and my year," said Dr. Wilson. "Thank you for reaching out to me. I am so happy that you're doing well."

Obviously, my behavior during our first meeting must have bothered him a lot, or he probably wouldn't have remembered my name.

"Oh, and I'm sorry I accused you of not being compassionate," I added. "I wasn't in my right mind."

"Don't worry about that. I'm just so glad you called me."

So was I.

Journal entry:

I am in the hospital for another chemo treatment and three-day slumber party at the Brigham. Oh, how I wish this Brigham was the Brighams Ice Cream shop of my childhood, with its spinning red counter stools and hot fudge sundaes that dripped warm chocolate all over the bottom of a silver dish. But no, this Brigham is about to fill my veins with yellow liquid with the hopes of keeping my tumors in remission, and I am grateful for it.

The Good C-Word

AFTER I HAD been in remission for quite a while, Dr. Norden asked to meet with Al and me in his office. We walked into the room and sat next to each other while he pulled a chair across from us.

"First of all, I want to say that you're doing awesome," he said. "But the fact is that with this chemo regimen alone, there is an 80 percent chance that you will have a recurrence before five years."

I hated hard facts, and he very rarely used them. What was up with this?

Al tried to come to the rescue. "But those relapse statistics are for people with poor immune systems, like AIDS patients, aren't they, Dr. Norden?"

"No, they're for everyone."

Al looked at me and shrugged as if saying, "Sorry, Ree, I tried."

Dr. Norden then told us about some new studies that were being conducted, mostly in Europe, where they were treating PCNSL patients with stem cell transplants.

"I can't quote statistics because it's all so new, but preliminary results have been very positive. We routinely treat relapsed cases of your lymphoma with a stem cell transplant here at Dana-Farber, but never people like yourself who are in first remission. I'm thinking that having this procedure now might increase your chances of a cure, Marie."

Dr. Norden's use of the good c-word gave me an incredible high, so I decided to give this option some serious thought. I took home a huge stack of medical documentation and booklets on the procedure.

The transplant would involve a three-and-a-half-week stay in isolation at the hospital while they harvested stem cells from my bloodstream, froze them in liquid nitrogen, and then blasted me with a high dose chemotherapy cocktail for about eight days. During this period of time, my body would have no immune system, and any kind of infection, even a bad tooth, could do me in. (Maybe I could get dentures ahead of time just to be on the safe side.) After this extended barrage of chemo, my stem cells would be put back in my body to "rescue" me and begin creating a whole new immune system. Side effects included baldness, mouth sores, nausea, and a twenty- to thirty-pound weight loss (the latter was not unappealing).

At the end of my research, I asked if I could speak to a stem cell transplant survivor, someone who had gotten the procedure after suffering a relapse of PCNSL. A sixty-three-year-old woman named Nancy agreed to speak with me. She was sixty days post-transplant and was back in her home.

"I'm not going to lie to you, Marie," she said. "It was the hardest thing I've ever done in my life. But am I glad I did it? Yes. Absolutely. It was my only shot at living."

"Was the isolation unit horrible?" I asked. "Did you miss your family and friends?"

"That wasn't as tough you would think," she said. "Most of the time I was feeling so sick that I wouldn't have wanted to see anyone. And I could call people on the phone and Skype them on the computer if I wanted to, which wasn't very often. Just dealing with the nausea was about all I could handle. But now I'm doing much better."

Nancy's report on what she went through made the whole thing real for me. A stem cell transplant wasn't just something written about in books and pamphlets; it was something that was being done to people who had to suffer through it. A few weeks later, I met with the head of the Dana-Farber's transplant team, a pretty young doctor with dark hair and sparkling blue eyes.

"You would be the only PCNSL patient in first remission to ever receive a transplant in our hospital or in the city of Boston," she said excitedly. "You would be breaking new ground." The term *guinea pig* flashed through my mind, but I quickly replaced it with *pioneer*.

After meeting with the transplant team, I was afraid but also oddly exhilarated at the thought of upping my chances of a cure. I took to the web to see if any results of the new clinical studies had been published. They hadn't, but one person's name kept appearing and reappearing every time I Googled the term *primary central nervous system lymphoma*. Dr. Linda Rinaldi was a prominent neuro-oncologist in New York and apparently the global guru on my disease.

Her publications and studies riddled the Internet like banner ads, so I resolved to set off to see this Wizard of PCNSL for a second opinion before I agreed to have the stem cell transplant. I was a little afraid to tell Dr. Norden that I wanted to meet with her, but he was completely fine with it and even encouraged me to go. He forwarded all my records and scans to her office immediately.

Lesson learned: Don't be afraid to ask for a second opinion. You need to be sure that the next step you take is the right one.

A Cure for PCNSL? LOL

BEFORE I COULD travel to New York, I had to go through another chemo treatment and three-day stay at the Brigham. I was sitting on my bed waiting to get discharged when Dr. Black, a tall woman wearing an ankle-length Tartan plaid skirt, came by on her rounds. I recognized her as a member of the hospital's transplant team, so I decided to get her thoughts.

"Dr. Norden seems very hopeful that if I have a stem cell transplant, I'd have a better chance of a cure," I said. "What do you think about that?"

"A cure for primary central nervous system lymphoma?" she said almost laughing. "I've never seen anyone cured of PCNSL for more than five years."

Her words shot through me like a lightning bolt.

"What do you mean?" I said, my eyes welling with tears. "No one ever gets cured?"

"Not in my experience," she said matter-of-factly. Then seeing how upset I was, she backtracked a bit. "Well, to be honest, I don't see that many patients with your illness. It's very rare."

As she left the room, she looked back at me from the doorway. "Are you going to be all right, Mrs. Fricker?"

"Apparently not," I said.

By the grace of God, Dr. Norden walked in just at that moment. "What happened?" he asked. "Why are you crying?

"I was telling that doctor about the transplant, and she said nobody gets cured of my disease for longer than five years."

"Dr. Black is not aware of the current statistics on PCNSL," he said angrily. "Wait a minute, I'll be right back."

I was wondering if he was going to try to catch her and say, "How dare you upset my patient like that?" But he returned in about ten minutes with a stack of papers in his hand. He had printed out a bunch of promising statistics about my illness on the computer at the nurse's station. I read them and felt a little better.

"Marie, can we make a deal?" he said, putting his hand out to shake on it. "Please don't talk about your case with anyone but me from now on. And that includes cafeteria personnel, patients, cleaning people, *and* other doctors."

"Okay," I said, but I didn't shake on it.

Off to See the Wizard

JAY CAME WITH Al and me to NYC for the second opinion visit with Dr. Rinaldi. We drove to the city in a spitting rain, arriving at our small Midtown hotel at 8:30 p.m. I looked at my son's glum face as we boarded the narrow, gray-walled elevator and thought of the many other trips to the Big Apple that Al and I had made with our kids through the years.

During those excursions, we had always clapped and cheered in the car as we caught the first sight of the New York City skyline in the distance. No matter how many times I'd seen it, the Empire State Building towering on the horizon always gave me a thrill. And then came the horn-blowing, bumper-to-bumper ride through the yellow taxi-ridden streets to our hotel.

We usually made the trip in December, when Macy's windows were alive with moving mannequins and toys and Rockefeller Center housed the majestic newly lit Christmas tree beside its sunken skating rink. The next day, we would take in the Rockettes holiday show at Radio City Music Hall and have dinner at the glittering Tavern on the Green.

These adventures were not cheap (about $1,500 for a weekend), and my coworker Debbie used to chastise me about the hefty price tag on our annual outings. "Marie, you're nuts to spend that kind of money," she'd say. "You're just mounting up thousands of dollars on charge cards when you should be saving for your retirement."

Ironically, Debbie called me after my brain tumor diagnosis and said, "I'm so sorry I gave you such a hard time about your trips to New York, Marie. Now I'm so glad you did that."

Her phone call was meant to be nice, but it convinced me that she, and most likely everyone else at Conway, had me dead and buried. I wondered how she would feel about this far less exciting adventure in NYC that I was currently engaged in.

We set three alarm clocks at the hotel so that we wouldn't miss our 7:30 a.m. appointment at the hospital. Arriving there in plenty of time, we were told to stop into the financial office, where a woman in a green uniform repeatedly asked, "Are you sure your insurance has approved this consultation?"

No matter how many times I said yes, she seemed unwilling to believe me. Finally, she pointed us in the direction of the fourth floor and the office of the esteemed Linda Rinaldi. I felt like I was about to meet with royalty, an all-knowing icon who would disclose the true cure for PCNSL and point me down the yellow brick road to wellness.

After a brief meet and greet with one of her associates, the door opened, and the wizard appeared. She was wearing a white lab coat, had short wavy hair and a sober expression, and appeared to be in her late forties. Al, Jay, and I got up from our seats to shake her hand. For me, that was a real effort because I was feeling like abject hell, both physically and emotionally.

"Before we begin, Doctor, may I have your permission to tape our conversation?" I asked. "I just want to be able to share it with Dr. Norden in case I forget something."

"I have no problem with that," she said as I put my tiny dictation machine on the table between us and hit Record.

"So you know why we're here," I said. "I would really like to get your opinion on whether or not I should have a stem cell transplant at this time."

"Mrs. Fricker, there have only been three studies on transplants for PCNSL patients who are in first remission," she said. "Two of them included brain radiation, and the other one was ours, and quite frankly, our results were not so hot. We have since changed our chemo regimen, and so far, people are doing well in the second study, but a stem cell transplant is always risky."

With that, she stopped talking, and I thought of Dorothy pleading with her wizard when he tried to dismiss her, "But please, sir, we've come so far."

I mustered up the courage to continue, even though this woman's presence was quite intimidating to me. She was a world-renowned brain cancer specialist and not very friendly. I was nervous but determined to get what I had come here for—advice from an expert on what to do next.

"So, Doctor, I just want to be clear that I've understood you correctly. Are you advising me not to get the stem cell transplant and to stick with my chemotherapy regimen at Dana-Farber?"

"You're putting words in my mouth," she said, looking over toward my husband and son as if willing them to haul me out of there. "If you are asking me what this hospital would do, we would not transplant you off protocol at this point in time. If they are offering this to you as an option in Boston, you will have to meet with your doctors and weigh the potential pros and cons for yourself."

"But do you think that my odds of a cure would be greater if I got it?" I persisted, wanting to grab her by the ankle and drag behind her until she told me everything she knew.

"Mrs. Fricker, I cannot tell you that a transplant will increase your chance of a cure from 20 to 40 percent, but nobody can," she said. "By definition, when you have a study, you don't know if it's the best way to go. That's the bottom line here. It was nice meeting you. I have to see another patient now. I wish you good luck."

"You too," I said as she left the room, and I turned off my tape recorder.

"She doesn't want you to have it, Mom," said Jay as we ate lunch in the hospital cafeteria after the consultation. "She's not going to come right out and say it, but that's what she was implying. Don't you think so, Dad?"

"Yes," said Al as he flipped open the lid on a metal soup canister to ladle clam chowder into a plastic bowl. "I don't think she wants you to quit the chemo and have a transplant now. Maybe if you get a relapse, but not now."

"I agree with you both," I said, sitting at an orange Formica table with a wobbly metal leg. "But I just wish she had come right out and said, 'No, I don't think you should have the stem cell transplant.'"

So as with Dorothy and her three traveling companions, my trip to Oz was somewhat anticlimactic. Like them, I would have to make my own decision about how to proceed working with my doctors in Boston because in my journey, too, there was no place like home.

I let Dr. Norden listen to the tape of my visit with the wizard at my appointment with him later that week.

"You actually recorded this?" he said, laughing. "I guess that figures."

After it ended, he said, "I'm not 100 percent sure she's saying that you shouldn't have the transplant. You may be misinterpreting things here."

A few days later, he stopped by my hospital room while I was playing Scrabble on my laptop after a chemo treatment. "I just got a follow-up letter from New York about your consultation," he said.

"Oh my god. What did she say? Was I right?"

"You were right. She's not in favor of a stem cell transplant for you at this time," he said. "I only brought it up, Marie, because the results of the first studies looked promising, and I so want to save you."

"I know that," I said. "That's what heroes do."

The End and the Beginning

I ULTIMATELY DECIDED not to get the stem cell transplant and to finish my chemotherapy regimen at the Dana-Farber. Bedside manner aside, the wizard of PCNSL was the leading expert on my disease, and I was going to take her advice.

I completed my thirteen months of chemo on December 10, 2009, and drove to the hospital alone for my final treatment. There was an odd joy and sadness to this day as I was untethered from my IV pole and disconnected for the last time from the healing but toxic liquid cursing to my veins from a brown-covered bag.

I drove home from the hospital in a weird state of relief mixed with fear of a future that didn't include monthly monitoring of my condition by medical experts. Was I capable of going it alone? At least before, I had structure, a routine. What now?

"Surprise," yelled Al and a group of neighbors when I got home to a front lawn decorated with silver and gold balloons. Ted leaned over the railing of his back deck and shouted, "Woo-hoo, Fearless Fricker!" I thanked everyone, gave some hugs, and then went into the house and sat at my kitchen table feeling more drained than exhilarated.

"Here, Ree, you do the honors," said Al, handing me a red magic marker and taking the giant *Boston Globe* calendar off the wall and putting it in front of me on the table. I drew an *X* on the block for December. There were twelve others preceding it, each painstakingly marked every month to show progress toward the goal of completing my treatments.

A few days later, I got an envelope in the mail from Dr. Norden. There was a light blue postcard inside with a smiling green frog in the upper left corner. In his familiar scrawl, he had written, "Congrats on finishing your chemo! I am looking forward to many, many years of uneventful follow-up visits." He had underlined *uneventful* to make me feel good. It worked.

I added the card to my stash of positive comments from him—the napkin notes and the scribbled quotes on the back of hospital menus, envelopes, and pages torn from celebrity magazines. They were all there, safely tucked away in the middle drawer of my mother's oak desk, which was now mine.

Lesson learned: It's normal to feel afraid when the medical treatment period ends. Switching from patient to survivor can be traumatic. But you will come to love it.

Merry Christmas

It was the tenth of December, and I was in the holiday spirit as almost never before. My brain was clear of its deadly lesions, and whether or not I was cured for now or forever, I was going to enjoy the moment.

The previous Christmas Eve, while Al and the kids had been attending our annual family bash at Harry and Lorraine's house, I had been lying in my bed facedown, unable to summon the strength to change from my sweat suit into pajamas. The sleeve was soothing the buzz in my left arm long enough to let me escape into the merciful respite of sleep.

Now just twelve months later, I was humming "Jingle Bells" while stringing white lights on the mantle and bugging Al to hang the wreaths on the windows.

During my battle with cancer, I had felt the presence of God spurring me on, holding me up, copiloting my car, and easing the fear of losing my life on a daily basis. I had not entered this illness as a devoutly religious person, but the evidence of a higher power playing a hand in my recovery was undeniable. I was never alone.

A nurse's aide in my early weeks at the hospital calmed me with my deceased mother's smile. I felt a hand in mine during a surgery when no human hand was near, and spiritual comfort came to my son in a parking garage. There was always the possibility that the young aide's resemblance to my mom was coincidental, that the conscious sedation during the port procedure created the illusion of someone stroking my hand, and that Jay was just imagining things, but I don't believe any of these scenarios. That's my choice and my solace.

High Heels On

JUST TWO WEEKS after my last chemo treatment, Jack Conway's daughter Carol Bulman called to offer me a part-time job as the head writer for the company. Declining in health and stamina, Jack had appointed Carol CEO of the firm on his eighty-sixth birthday. She was smart and savvy and a worthy successor to the throne.

"Would you consider coming back to work for us three days a week, Marie?" she asked. "We have some big projects coming up, and we could really use your writing skills."

"I'm grateful for the offer, Carol," I said. "But I don't think I have the stamina to do it."

"Couldn't you just give it a try? If you find that three days is too much for you, you can always cut it back to two."

"Okay, I'll try it," I said, hanging up the phone, feeling totally unsure of myself and my abilities.

On my first day back at work, I wore high heels—my leopard-print stilettos—for the first time since the night of Ben's birth. I had always been a shoe fanatic, so this was a big step back to normalcy. I put a framed photo of my mother on my desk for support, as well as one of Sue Haigh, who had recently lost her long battle with breast cancer. The last time

I had seen Sue was a few weeks before I returned to Conway. She had been sitting at her desk surrounded by mounds of paperwork as usual.

"I'm in real trouble this time, Marie," she said, wearing a brown wig, which meant she was getting chemo again. "I feel like I'm on the show *Survivor*, and they're voting me off the island, and I don't want to go.

"Oh, you'll pull through this, Sue," I said. "You always do."

One week later, she passed away peacefully at the same hospital that had saved my life.

Jack Conway had officially retired from his business in 2010, but he never really left the company until he left the world in the summer of 2012. Even when he was getting radiation treatments for advanced stage melanoma, he would stop into headquarters on his way home.

On one of these days, he called me into his office, where he was sitting in his red leather chair, dictating a letter into a pocket tape recorder. He ended the message with a final "Jack out" and asked me to have a seat across from him.

"You know, they tell me I have cancer, Marie," he said. "I'm not afraid of dying because I'm good with the Lord, but I'd really rather stick around."

Jack's phone rang at that moment, so I left his office quickly with my eyes filled with tears. When he died a few months later, the line of mourners at his wake stretched out of St. Mary's Church in Scituate Harbor and almost a quarter of a mile down the street beside it. It was the hottest day of the year, and hundreds of people stood in the sun for hours as they waited to pay their last respects to a man that each of them considered a personal friend.

I missed Jack's larger-than-life presence at work for a long while, but I was grateful to Carol for offering me the part-time job as a writer. A lot of CEOs wouldn't have hired a brain tumor survivor for any task, but this leader had risk-taking in her genes, and like her father, she was not afraid.

Afterthoughts

So NOW THIS chapter of my story ends. I have been to the bottom of the well. I have heard the laughter at the surface where real-world people were living real lives while I could only stretch out my hand to beg them to pull me up.

And when the ladder was lowered down the dark shaft, I climbed it, one rung at a time, sometimes slipping back a step or two but always pushing forward, keeping my eye fixed on the sliver of light that knifed through the blackness leading the way out.

I had brain cancer, but my head is clear and my life is intact. The neuropathy on my left side is still there, and every once in a while, I still get the urge to stick my left foot into a bucket of ice water, but only when it's been sitting too long in the hot tub at the nail salon where my toes and fingers are once again adorned in the bright-pink shade of Madison Mauvenue.

When I went for my six-month MRI with Dr. Norden in November of 2014, he entered the room with his usual right thumb in the air. "It looks great," he said, smiling. "Now guess what I'm going to say to you?"

"I don't know," I said, looking at Al, who had come with me to the appointment. (He had recently retired and was much more attentive.)

"I'll see you in a year," said Dr. Norden. "I'm cutting the umbilical cord, and you can get your chemo port removed."

I touched the bumpy spot that my port inhabited in my chest, and I dared to ask, "Do you think I could possibly be [I was so afraid to say the word] cured?"

"I think you are cured," he said, flashing the same perfect smile that had pulled me out of the fetal position on the day we met.

"Thanks for saving my life, Doogie Howser," I said.

"It was my pleasure!"

Marie's Top 15 List

Like former *Late Night* TV host David Letterman's Top Ten List, here are the top 15 things I learned from having cancer.

1. Love is most important.
   Having the love and support of friends and family is everything when you're fighting the fight. Also, it helps to hug. Going from an uptight "non-toucher" to someone who gives and receives hugs feels great.

2. Ask questions.
   Be aware of your own treatment, including medications. Don't assume the doctors and nurses always have it right. If you know you are supposed to get a pink pill and suddenly it's yellow, ask why.

3. If you look better, you feel better.
   Don't wear a johnny if you're an inpatient for an extended period unless you can't dress yourself. Bring some nice pajamas or yoga pants with you. The blue-and-white checked hospital gown has a way of lowering your IQ by fifty points. I once had a roommate who wore a johnny the entire time I knew her, trudging back and forth to the bathroom in paper slippers. One

day, I asked her what kind of work she did. She said, "I'm a superintendent of schools." I was shocked. They tell you to dress for success in the business world. Dress for wellness in the hospital world.

4. Keep a journal.
   Record your cancer journey from start to finish. If you don't feel like writing when you're having a bad day, that's fine. It's not a chore, but it does help to put your thoughts and fears on paper.

5. Like your oncologist.
   This person is your new best friend. He or she is not infallible, but if you don't feel a huge sense of trust and admiration for your doctor, find a new one.

6. Take your meds.
   At first, it was hard for me to carry around a suitcase of multicolored pills for daily use, but I got used to it. Before I got cancer, I didn't do drugs, but with cancer, drugs did me, and they did me good—not only the life-saving chemotherapy but the antianxiety medication that made the journey more tolerable. If you are suffering mentally, you may suffer more physically. Here is a link to a December 2015 blog from the Dana-Farber. It explains this tip better than I can: http://blog.dana-farber.org/insight/2015/12/how-medications-for-mood-and-anxiety-can-benefit-cancer-patients/.

7. Find a local cancer support group.
   This is a place where you don't have to put on a brave face. Your friends and family will listen to your fears

and endless litany of symptoms, but they will weary after a while. The people in your support group won't because they are in the trenches with you.

8. Keep busy.

   No matter how bad I felt, I did things, even if it was just checking my e-mail or getting someone to take me for a drive. Those early rides were a godsend, to see the sun and look from the car window at normal people doing normal things. It's good to be in the noncancer world even for a little while.

9. Pray.

   I prayed silently and out loud for the strength to make it through another day or for relief from a certain pain or symptom. As a Catholic, I prayed to God, Jesus, and the Blessed Mother. But whatever your beliefs may be, faith in a power higher than yourself can bring you solace.

10. Set your goal on bedtime.

    This advice came from a school nurse named Sheila who works with my daughter. She called me one night to see how I was doing. I told her I could barely make it through the day and that all I ever looked forward to was going to sleep at night to escape the misery. She said, "Then make that your goal. Don't think about tomorrow or next week, just think about surviving until bedtime." It worked for me.

11. Don't Google your illness.

    It's fine to check Facebook or play Words with Friends, but don't search for your illness on the Internet. The statistics may scare you more than the disease, and most of them are out of date. Trust me, your doctors know more than WebMD.

12. Remember, it's temporary.

After I had the allergic reaction to my second dose of chemo, I told my friend Joyce that I couldn't go back for the third treatment. "Yes, you can," she said. "Even if it's as bad as it was last time, you know that in three days, you'll be back on your couch holding your dog again. You can endure anything for three days." She was right.

13. Write the good stuff down.

Write down any positive, encouraging statements from your doctor and read them back later when you need them.

14. Bring coping devices.

If you have to be in the hospital for an extended period, bring your tablet or laptop, your cell phone, earplugs, and an eye mask. You'll keep your mind active and be able to sleep in a noisy environment.

15. Personalize your hospital room.

Bring your favorite blanket, pillow, and some framed family photos. When you wake in the night and see your things around you, you won't feel as much like a stranger in an alien land.

And above all else, when you hear the words, "You have cancer," remember, your life isn't over; you just have to fight for it.

Fifteen Minutes of Fame

SINCE I ENDED my chemo treatments in 2009, I've had the chance to share my story with some interesting audiences. Dr. Norden invited me to appear with him on the annual Jimmy Fund WEEI telethon in August of 2011. I met him at the Dana-Farber, and we took a shuttle over to Fenway Park, home of the World Champion Red Sox, where the event was taking place.

"Now this is what I always wanted," I said, settling into a seat next to him in the trolley. "To hang out with my friend Andrew on the weekend."

He laughed but looked a little uncomfortable. In the back of his mind, he was probably thinking, *Could she be a stalker?*

When we got to the park, we were interviewed on radio and TV, where I raved about the man and the hospital that had saved my life. I also talked about the little girl I had seen in the Jimmy Fund Clinic on my walk over the bridge that day.

"How did it make you feel when you saw that sick child?" asked WEEI sports radio host Gerry Callahan, holding a microphone to my mouth. "How important do you think it is for people to contribute to this Jimmy Fund telethon today?"

"When I saw that little girl, it really put my own illness into perspective," I said, sitting next to Dr. Norden during the live broadcast in a glass-fronted suite above Fenway Park. "She couldn't have been more than five years old. She hadn't even lived yet. I urge everyone who is listening to this telethon today to give from their hearts. My family and I will be walking in the Jimmy Fund Marathon this year as a way of saying thanks to the Dana-Farber Cancer institute for giving me a second chance at life."

When I got to work on the day after the telethon, I had celebrity status, even though I was mortified to see how fat and frumpy I had looked sitting next to glamorous blond sportscaster Jade McCarthy during the NESN TV interview.

"How did you have the nerve to talk so easily in front of those cameras?" said Kelly, biting into a sesame bagel at her desk. "I never could have done that."

"Are you kidding me? I loved it," I said. "I've always wanted to be a talk show host, so I got my fifteen minutes of fame. Took a trip to hell and back to get it, but it is what it is."

The After-Party

IN THE SPRING of 2010, I decided to throw a party to thank everyone in my life who had supported me during my brain cancer journey. Al's brother Harry and his wife, Lorraine, hosted the reception, which was held on a Saturday night in their entertainment room, with its floor-to-ceiling palladium windows and French doors leading to their pool and gardens.

Invitations went out to all the people who had lent a hand, physically or emotionally in my battle—family, friends, neighbors, members of my cancer support group, and my Conway colleagues.

The guest of honor, however, was the hardest to convince.

"Will you come to the party, Dr. Norden?" I asked, during one of my appointments with him for an MRI.

"Oh, I don't know, Marie," he said. "I've never done anything like that before with a patient."

He was big on not crossing the line from doctor-patient to personal friend, and I think he was again thinking "possible stalker."

"Oh, come on, you have to come, Dr. Norden. You're the guest of honor," I said. "Everybody wants to meet you.

I promise I won't try to friend you again on Facebook if you come to my party."

"Okay, that's a deal," he said, laughing. "Can I bring my wife?"

"Of course."

Dr. Norden and his petite dark-haired wife, Pam, arrived at the house right on time. He was wearing a striped button-down shirt and dark jeans—so odd not to see him in his usual white coat and stethoscope.

"Oh geez, I'm underdressed," he said, looking around the room.

"No, you're not," I said. "You look fine—out of character, but fine."

Three waitresses wearing black pants, white blouses, and red bow ties passed trays of wine and hors d'oeuvres as people mingled in the big room. A poster (designed by Kelly and Debbie) showing two photographs of me—one when I was sick and looking desolate and one of me smiling and recovered—was on a gold easel in the middle of the room. The word "*HOPE*" ran across the middle of it. Kelly had wanted to use the words "Stand up to Cancer," the new power slogan that was being touted on TV fund-raisers," but I couldn't. The fact was I had never stood up to cancer. Cancer had taken me down to my knees, and I had literally crawled my way back from it.

As Harry dimmed the lights, everyone sat around a big screen TV in the center of the room and watched the telethon interview of Dr. Norden and me. When it was over, using a hand microphone (yes, I actually owned one), I thanked all my guests for the love and support they had shown me through the journey.

When I got to Jack Conway (the party took place right before he was diagnosed with cancer), I asked him if he would like to say a few words because I knew there was no occasion at which he would not want to address an audience. "Sure I would," he said, leaning on his leopard-print cane and walking to the middle of the room.

Taking the mike from my hand, Jack cajoled the crowd as only he could do and wound up his remarks with these words. "I just want to say that we were all heartbroken when we heard that Marie had a brain tumor. But then she met this good doctor here, and she asked him, 'Dr. Norden, can you help me?' and he said, 'Madam, I not only can help you, I can cure you.'"

He was, of course, exaggerating, but everyone cheered, and Jack resumed his seat next to his wife, Patti, on the couch. I looked over at the guest of honor, who was shifting in his chair and looking a little flushed. He was definitely feeling uncomfortable.

"Thanks so much, Jack, for your comments," I said. "And now I'd like to introduce everyone to the person who made this little victory celebration possible. His name is familiar to you all since I've talked about him incessantly for the last eighteen months. Please welcome the man who saved my life, my hero, Dr. Andrew Norden."

My guests rose to their feet applauding and whistling as Dr. Norden joined me at the front of the room and took the microphone.

"Well, I guess you all do know my name," he said, laughing. "I'm Andrew Norden, a neuro-oncologist at the Dana-Farber Cancer Institute and certainly not a hero. It was Marie who did all of the hard work. I just want to say that it is a pleasure to meet the entire 'Team Fricker' that was behind the scenes, supporting my patient in the trenches."

After Dr. Norden spoke, I ended the evening by announcing a special award. "On every team, there is a most valuable player, and this one is no different," I said. "I would now like to honor the individual who saw me through my brain tumor battle from day 1 until today and without whom, I would not be standing here tonight."

I peeled open an envelope and read from it. "The MVP award in Marie Fricker's battle against PCNSL goes to her son, Jason Henry Fricker."

Jay, who is beyond shy, flushed scarlet, on his bar stool at the back of the room next to his fiancée, Kim. He stood up and waved to everyone and said, "Thanks, Ma," and sat back down on his stool with the blush just starting to recede from his cheeks.

"Oh no, you're not getting off that easy," I said. "You have to come up here to get your prize."

People were chanting "Go, Jay!" so he reluctantly joined me at the front of the room, where he stiffly submitted to a hug. I presented him with a $100 gift certificate to his favorite restaurant and then proceeded to embarrass him even further as I read a story I had written about him during one of my chemo treatments.

My Son—My Solace

When you give birth to a child, it's one of the most exciting moments of your life, but what they lay in your arms as you sink back into the hospital pillow is a tiny blob of humanity. Yes, he has your eyes and your father's right dimple, but he is a stranger who must ingratiate himself into your family and your heart in the months and years that follow.

There are times when he exasperates you, as you hover over him, begging for completion of a homework assignment. Or when his junior high school teacher calls you in to discuss your son's acting-out behavior.

You laugh and say, "Oh, he's just the class clown," but she isn't amused.

And then one day, he graduates as the number 1 firefighter recruit in the state of Massachusetts, and you clap and cry and forget all the foibles of his teenage years. And then he learns his mother has cancer and will need seventeen chemo treatments over fourteen months.

And he rearranges his work schedule and uses all his vacation time so he can drive her to the Dana-Farber and sit by her side. He doesn't hold her hand—he's not a toucher—and besides, he says, "You don't need that. Things are going great. They're going to cure you."

He buys several books on the power of prayer and positive thinking and leaves them behind on her nightstand. "Read these, they're good," he says, with a smile that shows her father's dimple.

The love and pride I have in this boy, who has become an incredible man, is impossible to describe. He is a firefighter (now a captain) and a paramedic who has saved many lives, including his mother's, who never would have made it through the battle without him."

Acknowledging Jay that night in front of everyone made me feel good. I wanted the world to know how much he had done for me and how much I appreciated him.

The Class Convenes

A COUPLE OF months after the party, Dr. Norden called and asked if I would be willing to talk about my illness with a group of fourth-year Harvard medical students who were coming to Dana-Farber to hear him discuss an unusual case.

"You can say no," he said. "But I think you would be really great at this."

"I'm in. Just tell me where and when. And will you validate my parking?"

I sat at the end of a long mahogany conference table while the students—some wearing white lab coats and stethoscopes, others in regular college kids clothes—lined each side of it. They took out pens, notebooks, and tablets and looked up at Dr. Norden, who was standing next to me at the front of the room.

"I would like to introduce you all to one of my favorite patients," he said.

"He says that about everyone," I said and got a few laughs.

"Marie, would you please tell the group about how you presented with your illness, the treatment you received, and the coping strategies that helped you?"

I told my story while two MRI scans of my brain were projected on a computer screen behind me.

"This is the original image showing the tumors in Marie's thalamus and frontal lobe," said Dr. Norden, tapping the white spots with a pointer. "And this is her latest MRI scan, which, as you can see, is completely clear."

I heard a couple of "wows," including my own.

At the end of our presentation, Dr. Norden asked if the students had any questions for me. One kid wearing a bright green bow tie asked, "Clinically speaking, have you been left with any deficits?"

"Yes, some," I admitted. "The neuropathy pain on my left side can be a ten on some days, but most of the time it's moderate. I have a permanent case of Novocaine lip, but I can walk, talk, work, and play. I may never be the precancer me again, but I don't care. I'm eternally grateful just to be."

The first session went so well that Dr. Norden asked me to do two more of them. I intentionally went for some laughs during each of our "dog and pony" shows, but I always stressed how much my doctor's caring nature helped to get me through the worst of times.

At the end of each class, I tried to make eye contact with every student at the table and say, "Please remember that you will not only be practicing medicine in your future careers, you will be lifelines for people who are feeling lost and afraid. Your patients will need your kindness and compassion every bit as much as your expertise."

I could tell just by looking at these smart and privileged young people that some of them were getting the message and some not. Ruling out the few who were actually dozing off (I attributed that to their exhaustion from medical school, not to my boring presentation), there were those who paid close attention, smiled, and nodded their heads with understanding. Others looked aimlessly around the room, stretched their necks and shoulders in their chairs, and swiftly headed out the door when the class was over.

Oh well, if I got through to even one of these future physicians who might someday treat a patient with Dr. Andrew Norden's touch, then it was worth it.

Epilogue

June 27, 2015

TODAY IS MY sixty-second birthday—seven years since my diagnosis with an inoperable brain tumor, and I am back to a routine I never would have dreamed possible. I babysit for my two whirlwind grandsons, Ben and his younger brother Will, twice a week and continue to work as Jack Conway's head writer on the other three days.

Jay and his wife, Kim, have given Al and me two more precious descendants, Christian James, and our first grand-daughter, Olivia Marie, who bears my name—thankfully not posthumously.

In October of 2008, I never believed I would see my newborn grandson take his first steps, and now I've seen him run the bases in Little League and ride the school bus to first grade.

I am extremely grateful to the Dana-Farber and the Brigham and Women's hospitals and their incredible teams of doctors, nurses, chaplains, psychologists, and social workers who treated me as a whole person, not just a patient. I thank the friends and family who jumped in the trenches with me when catastrophe struck, as well as those who stood on the sidelines, tossing in supplies.

I try to remember the things that cancer taught me— to value every day as an incredible gift, to take nothing for granted (not even the drive-through lane at Dunkin' Donuts), and to comfort others when they're hurting.

We celebrated a family landmark a few weeks ago when my grandson Ben, six, swam in the deep end of my sister's in-ground pool for the first time. Alli and I had been urging him to do it for hours because we knew he was ready, but every time we'd ask, he'd wrap his purple noodle around him tightly and hug closer to the stairs.

"Come on, Ben, just give it a try," I said for the umpteenth time that day. "I'll go with you."

"Nooo, Nunny," he whined. "I'm too scared."

And then, with no warning, Benjamin James Kieffner put his head in the water and propelled himself across the turquoise surface of the pool like a sleek sunfish. I swam next to him the whole way, afraid that we may have pushed him too soon, but he made it to the other end with ease and repeated the feat several more times as we clapped and cheered.

When I was drying him off on the cement patio afterward, I kneeled down and looked into his crystal blue eyes with their flattened wet lashes. "You can swim, Benji!" I said, kissing his cold cheek and swaddling him in his thick red Spiderman towel. "Tell me something, buddy, why did you finally get the guts to do it?"

Through chattering teeth and purple lips, he said, "Because you were by my side."

Every day in every way, I'm getting better and better.

Survival

by Marie Fricker

The intruder crept up silently
Like a burglar in the night.
And when it struck its stealthy blow,
At first we shook with fright.

It slapped us down and made us moan
But when the tears were dry
We struggled up and faced the foe
And no more questioned why.

The battle waged, we took some blows
And hoped for a tomorrow
But certain gifts were hidden there
Beneath the pain and sorrow

A clearer view of God's great gifts
The value of each hour
We watched our spirits start to lift
We saw our inner power

Our doctors helped us fight the fight
The battle of our life
But cancer gave us new insight
Along with all the strife

To understand the treasures
Of a perfect starry night
To sit along a rocky coast
And watch a seagull's flight

To be with those we love the most.
Surrounded by their care.
The intruder crept upon us
But yes, we are still here.

Marie Fricker

Some Suggested Reading Materials That Helped Me Cope with Having Cancer

Groopman, Jerome. 2005. *The Anatomy of Hope: How People Prevail in the Face of Illness.* New York, New York: Random House.

Carr, Kris. *Crazy Sexy Cancer Survivor.* Guilford, Connecticut: Skirt.

Carr, Kris. *Crazy Sexy Cancer Tips.* Guilford, Connecticut: Skirt.

Silver, Julie K., ed. *What Helped Get Me Through: Cancer Survivors Share Wisdom and Hope.* American Cancer Society, Library of Congress.

Anderson, Greg. 1999. *Cancer: 50 Essential Things to Do.* New York, New York: Plume, a member of Penguin Group.

Osteen, Joel. *Hope Now*, a CD set. Houston, Texas: Joel Osteen Industries.

American Cancer Society. 1997. *Informed Decisions: The Complete Book of Cancer Diagnosis, treatment, and Recovery.* New York: Viking.

Anderson, Greg. (1988). *The Cancer Conqueror.* Andrews and McMeel.

Mantell, Susie. *Your Present: A Half-Hour of Peace: A Guided Imagery Meditation for Physical and Spiritual Wellness.*

Resources for the PCNSL Patient

PCNSL Peer-to-Peer Support Group: A comprehensive site for Primary Central Nervous System Lymphoma information–http://www.pcnsl.info/.

Central Nervous System Lymphoma (PCNSL) Friendship and Support Group (I Survive Brain Tumors) on Facebook. Search and ask to join the closed group.

PCNSL Real Life Stories: Stories from nine survivors and three primary caregivers. http://www.pcnsl.info/PCNSLe-book.pdf.

The American Brain Tumor Association: http://www.abta.org. An excellent list of financial resources and more.

The National Brain Tumor Society: http://www.braintumor.org.

Journal of Clinical Oncology: Primary Central Nervous System Lymphoma: A Curable Brain Tumor–http://jco.ascopubs.org/content/21/24/4471.full.

National Cancer Institute: Primary CNS Lymphoma Treatment: http://www.cancer.gov/cancertopics/pdq/treatment/primary-CNS-lymphoma/Patient/page4/AllPages\.

Article in The Oncologist May 2009 vol. 14–Primary CNS Lymphoma in Immunocompetent Patients–http://theoncologist.alphamedpress.org/content/14/5/526.full#sec-12.

Neurology Now magazine (free subscription) from the American Academy of Neurology–http://journals.lww.com/neurologynow/pages/subscriptionservices.aspx.

Caring Bridge: You can share your PCNSL journey with family and friends electronically by starting a page on Caring Bridge. http://www.caringbridge.org/.

Cancer.Net: Lymphoma–Non-Hodgkin: Treatment Options–http://www.cancer.net/cancer-types/lymphoma-non-hodgkin/treatment-options?sectionTitle=Treatment.

American Association of Hematology: Central Nervous System Lymphoma: http://asheducationbook.hematology library.org/content/2002/1/283.full.

Cancer.org: The American Cancer Society's most comprehensive online resource listing facts about specific diseases, tips for staying healthy, finding support and treatment, and exploring the latest research.

If you would like to help…

The department of neuro-oncology's research at the Dana Farber Cancer Institute focuses largely on clinical trials for new treatments of primary brain tumors. It was Dr. Norden's clinical knowledge, along with his compassionate care, that saved my life. This would not have been possible without the generosity and support of others. Please consider making an online gift to help find a cure for brain cancer at www.myjimmyfundpage.org/give/AllInMyHead.